What Color Is Your Parachute?

GUIDE TO
JOB-HUNTING ONLINE

What Color Is Your Parachute?

GUIDE TO

JOB-HUNTING ONLINE

6TH EDITION

MARK EMERY BOLLES and
RICHARD NELSON BOLLES

TEN SPEED PRESS
Berkeley

Copyright © 2011 by Mark Emery Bolles and Richard Nelson Bolles

Some of the material in this work appeared in somewhat different form in the
previous edition published as *Job-Hunting Online, 5th Edition,* by Ten Speed Press,
Berkeley, 2008.

Published in the United States by Ten Speed Press, an imprint of the Crown
Publishing Group, a division of Random House, Inc., New York.
www.crownpublishing.com
www.tenspeed.com

Ten Speed Press and the Ten Speed Press colophon are registered trademarks of
Random House, Inc.

Library of Congress Cataloging-in-Publication Data

Bolles, Mark Emery, 1955–
  What color is your parachute? : guide to job-hunting online : career sites, cover
letters, gateways, getting interviews, job search engines, mobile apps, networking,
niche sites, posting resumes, research sites, and more / Mark Emery Bolles,
Richard N. Bolles. — 6th ed.
      p. cm.
  Rev. ed. of: Job-hunting online / Mark Emery Bolles and Richard Nelson Bolles.
5th. ed.
  Includes index.
  1. Job hunting—United States—Computer network resources. 2. Web sites—
United States—Directories. I. Bolles, Richard Nelson. II. Bolles, Mark. Job-hunting
online. III. Title.
  HF5382.75.U6B65 2011
  025.06′65014—dc22
                          2010051035

ISBN 978-1-60774-033-9

Printed in the United States

Cover design by Katy Brown
Interior design by Betsy Stromberg

10 9 8 7 6

Sixth Edition

CONTENTS

Chapter 1

INTRODUCTION

ALL JOBS ARE TEMPORARY.

There is no promise made today that cannot be erased with an apology tomorrow. Companies go out of business, mergers occur, divisions are reorganized, projects get cancelled, funding is cut . . . and we're really sorry, but we're going to have to let you explore other opportunities.

Or maybe your company has grown uncomfortably large (or uncomfortably small); perhaps you have realized that the job you started with is not quite the same as the one you ended up with, and it's time to move on. Or your spouse has been promoted to a new area of the country. Or you took this last job knowing that it was only a two-year project, and it's time to look for the next one.

Figures vary, but most experts (and the federal government) say that the average job lasts three and a half years. Which means that the average person becomes a job-hunter every three and a half years, voluntarily or not. And the trend, on average, is toward shorter job tenures, not longer.

At the same time, it's taking each of us longer to find a job. In a trend that has been building for years, the US Bureau of Labor Statistics says that in April of 2009, the average job-hunt lasted just under twenty-seven weeks; less than a year later, in April of 2010, it was thirty-three weeks. For older workers seeking senior positions, the job-hunt (again, on average) generally takes between one and two *years*.

What is going on here? It's not like there aren't any jobs available. People are always quitting, being terminated, retiring, moving to another town . . . the turnover is endless. Even in the brutal economic times we have been going through, this country has shown a net job growth every year since 2001. I don't want to keep bombarding you with numbers, but in 2007 alone, although there were 54.6 million "separations"—that's government-speak for quits, layoffs, discharges, and retirements—employers hired 57.8 million people, for a net jobs gain of 3.2 million. Meaning, that every month, over 1 million people were finding jobs—158,000 people every day. But, on average, *it took them each over six months to find that job.*

This makes no sense. Every day, there are more jobs available; as time goes by, we have to go job-hunting more often; and yet, we are getting worse at it. You would think we'd be getting better, seeing as we need to do it so often. But all of the numbers point the other way.

Well, numbers can hide as much as they can reveal, but I do know one thing: this country is going through a revolution in the way the job-hunt operates. And one of the main factors in this revolution—perhaps even the main cause of the revolution—is the Internet.

As a job-hunter, you need to understand the Internet and know how to use it effectively in your job-hunt. If you can do that—learn how the Internet can help you find work, how it cannot, and even learn how the Internet will likely be harmful to your job-hunt—then you are no longer the average job-hunter that we have been talking about. Your search can take much less than thirty weeks, or whatever the average happens to be right now. You can, in a relatively short time, find the work you enjoy at a place you enjoy doing it. And that's the whole point of this book.

Monster Expectations

First let's look at some ways that the Internet is *not* helpful, and is perhaps even harmful, when you are job-hunting.

The first problem the Internet brings is unrealistic expectations. Many people think that the Internet will make the whole job-hunting process much easier and quicker. We are constantly bombarded with ads on TV, radio, in the newspaper, and on the Internet itself, all of which tell us that we merely have to put our resume up on one job site or another (the bigger the better) and we will soon be bombarded with job offers. For the vast majority of people, that is the complete sum of all they know about online job-hunting. It's simple; it's painless; what do I need a book like this for?

Unfortunately, Internet job-hunting just doesn't work that way. I'll explain more in chapter 2, but, for now, just know that when job-hunters follow these ads and only use what I call the Supersites (Monster, HotJobs—now part of Monster—and CareerBuilder), the average success rate is around 4%.

BLOGS

More often than not, a blog is a short article, published on a more-or-less consistent basis somewhat like a newspaper column. The blogosphere is the name given to the virtual world that contains all of the blogs ever written, about everything.

Most blogs are generated by a single person and will tend to be on the same subject, but not always. Some people write blogs, subject no obstacle, simply as a way of scratching whatever mental itch they happen to have that day.

It will come as no surprise that the best blogs are written by authorities in their fields, about their fields. But in a staggering number of cases, a blogger may appear to be writing for no reason other than to affirm that he can hear his own voice. Choose wisely.

That is, for every 100 people who use the Supersites, 4 people will find a job . . . eventually. The remaining 96 people never will.

The next problem facing the online job-hunter is data smog—the huge amount of information on the Internet tends to mask the information you are searching for. And the actual amount of information online is staggering: as of 2009, about 109 million different websites, with over 25 billion (yes, that's billion-with-a-"b") separate web pages. Great! Now—which ones are going to be helpful?

Well, let's try and cut through that data smog and zero in on our intended subject—that's what search engines are for, right? So we go to a typical search engine, such as Google, Yahoo, or Bing, and type in "job-hunting." Google alone claims about 23 million results and generally shows the first thousand (about 100 results pages). Of those thousand, which are the most helpful links for *your* job-hunt? If you think the answer is always on the first page— which is as far as most people go—then you need to learn a *lot* more about search engines. We'll examine search engines closely in chapter 6, Research.

That brings us to the third problem facing the online job-hunter: data provenance. We already know there is a huge amount of information on the Internet; it doesn't take long to find out that much of this information is vague, contradictory, and often just plain wrong. What, and who, are we to believe?

For example: In the last few years, there has been an explosion in the number of job-hunting blogs. Back in 2007, when I wrote the previous edition of this book, there were exactly *three* job-hunting blogs on the net. Now, just a few years later, there are literally thousands of job-hunting blogs. *Thousands*. It's bad enough having too much information. But now the question becomes: is it likely that every one of these bloggers is a job-hunting expert?

It used to be that we could (and did) trust what we read. The books, newspapers, and magazines that were our primary sources of information were generally produced by well-trained people with knowledge, experience, and authority. Generally speaking, journalistic professional pride and economic pressures required careful research, caution, and fact checking.

But the web is completely egalitarian. Anyone can set up a website and say whatever they want, as loud as they want, regardless of the truth of the matter or the depth of their knowledge about it. Without a great deal of expertise on *our* part, it can be difficult to distinguish the expert from the fraud, or the well-meaning but mistaken voice from the sharp operator who wants to cloud an issue for financial gain. Therefore, when on the Internet, you must constantly ask yourself:

- Where does the information come from?
- Who wrote it?
- Why did they write it?
- Why is it worth money to keep it available on the Internet?
- How can I verify this information?

These questions may not be so important when you are trying to find out who was our eighteenth president (Buchanan, unfortunately), but when you are trying to find work in a hostile world, such questions can be absolutely critical.

To illustrate the care required when using the Internet, I bring you the story of dihydrogen monoxide.

DHMO—A Cautionary Tale

There is a chemical compound affecting the health of people all over the world, yet it seems as if no one wants to talk about it.

Dihydrogen monoxide—often referred to as DHMO—is now widespread throughout our environment. A major component of acid rain, DHMO also contributes to soil erosion and the greenhouse effect. High levels of DHMO can be found in practically every lake and river in the US.

By going to the web page of the Dihydrogen Monoxide Research Division (www.dhmo.org/), we can learn that:

- Inhaling even a small amount of DHMO can cause death.
- The gaseous form of DHMO can cause severe burns on human skin.
- Prolonged exposure to solid DHMO causes severe tissue damage.
- To quote the website, "DHMO is a constituent of many known toxic substances, diseases and disease-causing agents, environmental hazards and can even be lethal to humans in quantities as small as a thimbleful."

More recently, concern has grown due to the fact that DHMO is being used widely on dairy farms, and is showing up in the milk that we give to our children.

Given all of these facts, why is so little being done to curb the use of DHMO? It's hard to know exactly why, given the close relationship between industry and people in politics. Some brave voices have been raised, but they are as those crying in the wilderness:

- A few years ago, the city councilors in Alisa Viejo, California, scheduled a vote on whether to ban Styrofoam cups at city events, because they learned that Styrofoam manufacture involves the use of DHMO.
- Some members of the New Zealand Parliament have thrown their weight behind efforts to curb the use of DHMO.
- In 2010, a member of the Canadian Parliament wrote a bill to ban DHMO from all federal buildings, though later tabled his bill (bowing to industry pressure?).

If you have any questions or concerns about DHMO, you should go to the website mentioned above, or to Wikipedia's excellent article on the subject at http://en.wikipedia.org/w/index.php?title=Dihydrogen_monoxide&redirect=no.

At this point, I should probably tell you that dihydrogen monoxide, or DHMO, is another way of saying H_2O, or water. And it is all true: water is a major component of acid rain; it causes soil erosion, and contributes to the greenhouse effect, particularly when it forms clouds. Breathing even small amounts will kill you, though we usually call it drowning; the gaseous form, known as steam, can cause burns; and prolonged direct exposure to the solid form (ice) causes tissue damage, known as frostbite. On dairy farms, they give it to the cows . . . somehow it works its way into the milk.

Okay, it's a fun little joke, but the politicians I mentioned above (and others) have actually been caught up in this hoax, most of which is centered around the DHMO web page.

Maybe it's built into our brains, or it's part of our education system. We tend to consider published information as generally trustworthy. When this trust is broken by magazines or newspapers—as with reporters Jayson Blair, Jack Kelley, and Stephen Glass, who famously plagiarized and fabricated news stories—it is major news itself.

But as our information sources migrate from paper publishing to the Internet, we need to remember that many of the old restraints just don't apply in the same way. On the Internet, you must always consider motivations, provenance, and expertise.

Much of this book will be devoted to steering you away from websites and job-hunting strategies I know to be inaccurate, a poor use of your time, or likely to cost you money. Instead, I'll try to point you to resources that will help you find work in the shortest time possible, and I'll show you how to research effectively online. I believe in empowerment: teaching you to fish is always better than giving you a fish.

The Benefits

Okay, we've talked about the net's problems; what's the flip side? What does the Internet have to offer the job-hunter?

Research: The huge amount of information available online, which in some ways is the Internet's weakness, is also its strength. The Internet is a researcher's dream, changing the way we approach learning and information. When was the last time you were at someone's house and saw a thirty-volume encyclopedia? All of the facts and materials we used to have to search for in heavy tomes, or go to the library to find, are now just a few mouse clicks away, available to anyone with a computer and an Internet connection (which *should* be every person who is actively job-hunting).

You can save a lot of time, and find a lot more information, if you understand how search engines work, how they differ, which search engines are best for certain tasks, and when search engines are not helpful. Moreover, much of the information on the web is not available through search engines at all. We'll look at other ways of finding online information later in the book.

Networking: When you are job-hunting, what you are really doing is looking for people. People with the power to hire you, people who work at a company that may have an opening for you, people who know that you are job-hunting and want to help, people who know that a certain company has a problem that you know how to fix . . . like that. Networking is people. A website is not an entity in itself; it is created and run by people. The Internet is just another form of communication between people. Communicating with people—what we like to call networking—is always the most successful way of finding a job.

There has been an explosion in the popularity of social-networking sites. Many people spend hours every day on sites such as Facebook and Twitter; you might even be one of them. If you are, your job-hunt will probably require you to change your habits.

Though there are effective ways to use the social-networking sites when looking for work, you don't need to spend hours at them every day. We'll talk about how to use these sites in your job-hunt, and which sites and strategies are the most effective. We'll also explore other ways of making contacts *and* reaching people on the Internet, and we'll talk about the fatal flaw that all social networking sites suffer from and how best to get around it.

Advice: There are people who are experts on job-hunting, and many offer their expertise to the job-hunter at no charge. Particularly, there are job-hunting sites that I call Gateways: websites, run by experts, that function as portals to the Internet for job-hunters, with many helpful articles and thousands of links to other sources of job-hunting information. Everything on these Gateway sites has already been vetted by experts. You don't

THE NET AND THE WEB

There was a time when the Internet was a series of different protocols, or methods of transmitting and receiving information, most of which are not much used directly anymore. Previous editions of this book dealt with protocols such as Listserv, Usenet, and FTP and explained their possible benefits to the job-hunter.

But we have come now to the point where the only part of the Internet that matters is the World Wide Web (and email, of course). If you are a true net expert, feel free to explore what benefits the older protocols may still have for your job-hunt, but there's really not much there when compared to the huge reach of the web. Therefore, throughout this book, I will be using the terms "Internet" and "World Wide Web" (as well as the short forms "net" and "web") pretty much interchangeably. For our purposes, they mean the same thing.

have to wonder if the information is good; it has already been tested and given their seal of approval. I'll show you the best Gateways and point out the weaknesses of others.

Resumes: To my mind, it is a tragedy, but none the less true: as the Internet has become more and more a part of the job-hunting process, the resume has gained more power. In many cases, the resume is the key that unlocks the employer's door. If your resume is just a bit off—if it is *really* close, but doesn't *quite* fit that lock—then you may be completely locked out of that job, unknown to the employer who (though he doesn't know it) is looking for *you*.

But not everyone translates well to paper. And there may be times when you *know* you can do a certain job, but how do you convince the prospective employer? The net has a lot to offer about resumes, how to write them, how to deliver them, and how to make them as effective as possible. We'll also look at ways of skirting the process a bit, and at nontraditional resume forms that may work better for you.

Job Boards: A simple contraction of "job bulletin board," these are websites where employers place job listings and job-hunters can post their resumes.

There are thousands of job boards on the net. You already know about the Supersites, but they are mostly a waste of time. Much better are the niche sites: the job boards that cater to people in certain lines of work, and the regionals, which are job boards that cater to people in a certain area. If you live in Seattle, what good is a job listing in Miami? It's just more dreck you have to dig through before you find something that might be useful, and you don't have the time to waste. We'll look at some good niche sites and regionals, and explore how to find helpful job boards on your own.

Many employers now prefer not to use job boards at all and, instead, list their job openings on the company's own website. How do we find those? It turns out that there are job search engines that go out to employers' websites and find the jobs listed there. We'll talk about these search engines and how best to use them. We'll also explore how to find companies, and their listed (and unlisted) job openings that the job search engines cannot find.

The Internet and Mobile Technology

You may have noticed that the line between computers and telephones is getting kind of fuzzy. The iPhone and iPad, Android, and other technologies are gaining more power all of the time. Often you can find "apps" (applications) that allow your smart phone to do many of the things your desktop or laptop computer does now. And in the coming years, you will start finding apps available for your car, your television, your refrigerator, your watch . . . anything with a microprocessor.

Currently, apps are a bit of a two-edged sword. They do allow your smart phone to perform special tasks, or use certain websites more efficiently; and many sites offer smart phone apps that are useful while job-hunting, such as Facebook, Twitter, LinkedIn, Indeed, Google . . . the list is growing every day.

But as I said, the sword has two edges. During the time you are using your CareerBuilder app, you are not using your Monster app. While using your Facebook app, you are not reading tweets. Even with multi-tasking operating systems, companies are finding that apps are a good way of reducing consumers' interaction with competitors. Said another way, using an app is, at least at some level, a tacit agreement by you to limit your own options. Moreover, apps make it easier for companies to gather data from and about *you*. That's not always to your benefit.

No one can predict what technology will bring in the coming years—I personally believe that laptop computers (if not all PCs) will eventually come to look and act very much like the iPad but it is a sure bet that there will be apps that allow your phone to do more and more of the things that your computer does, and at least some of these apps will be designed for job-hunters.

If you find that using smart phone apps makes your job-hunt more effective, go for it. But you may find that you will work more effectively if you conduct your job-hunt from one machine, at one location; usually your primary computer. No doubt your smart phone can help you when you are not at that primary location, but if you find yourself spending a lot of time transferring data from one machine to another, or cursing because a certain file is not where you need it to be, then you might want to rethink your strategy when it comes to using mobile technology in your job-hunt.

Using This Book

Throughout this book, I've listed the URLs of various websites that may be helpful to you. I do not expect you to visit every one of them; nor should you try. Read the descriptions of the sites I have listed, and use the ones that seem likely to be helpful.

As you visit these sites, you will quickly find that not only is it a pain to enter URLs (the site's web address) into a web browser, but it is also easy to make mistakes as you type. To solve this problem, you may want to go to this book's companion website at

http://job-huntingonline.webs.com/

where you will find hyperlinks to all of the sites listed in this book. From there you can just click on the link to any site you want to visit (or download the list of links to your own computer), and thereby avoid the laborious typing of URLs.

At this point, you may be tempted to jump right in and start clicking around at the various websites in the book. But do yourself a favor: temper any tendencies toward haste and read the book first. There is far more here than just a bunch of websites.

And speaking of websites: although I have included hundreds of excellent websites in this book, new ones are being created all the time. If you aren't finding what you need at the sites I recommend, or are curious about what sites may have been created after this book was published, then spend some time using the various suggestions under the "And Try These Search Terms" sections sprinkled throughout the book. Bear in mind that each of these lists should be considered incomplete, and nothing more than a starting point for your own imagination.

EMAILS AND TEXTS

As an example of the blurring between computers and phones, did you know that every cell phone (with text capability) has an email address? The address is based on the phone number and the carrier; so for example, to send a text to an AT&T cell phone whose number is (201) 555-1212, the email address would be 2015551212@txt.att.net.

Each carrier has a different address, but the format is always the same. Most carriers' addresses are listed at http://www.mutube.com/projects/open-email-to-sms/gateway-list/, and in most cases, you can find the carrier from the phone number alone by going to http://fonefinder.net/.

This email-to-text capability only works in one direction (to the phone, not from it), and all of the limitations of texting apply, such as message length. Still, it's a convenient way of sending short messages from your computer, or of transferring contact information from your computer to your phone.

And since websites themselves are constantly changing, see chapter 8 for what to do when URLs appear to have changed, or descriptions in this book don't match what you are finding online.

Book Updates

The net is constantly changing; links change, pages move, and with some protocols, a web page's URL is not the same for all users at all times. So if you find a URL that doesn't work or are sure the information you need just isn't where I said it should be, please let me know through the Job-Hunting Online website.

In spite of my spending more time than I want to think about on the Internet, I'm certain there are a lot of good sites about which I know nothing—not yet, anyway. If you find a site that was particularly useful to you in your job-hunt, and you think it should be listed in the next edition of this book, please let me know through the Job-Hunting Online site.

Chapter 2

FIRST

THE LAST HALF OF THE TWENTIETH CENTURY has seen many changes that have influenced the way we look for work in our society; the Internet is just the most recent. In fact, most of the job-hunting methods that we now use have evolved since World War II—a time when moving from one part of the country to another, and particularly the migration toward cities, became commonplace. Increases in population, along with this trend towards urbanization, made it more and more necessary to interact with complete strangers, with people that we didn't (yet) know. When you look at the job-hunt, and the different ways to go about it, you'll notice that what you are seeing is a people search as much as a work search. Stated simply, the ultimate goal of your job-hunt is to find the right person to hire you.

Obviously, there is more than one way to conduct this search. Changes in technology, society, and the world of work itself, have called for changes in the way we go about the job-hunt. As time goes on, new methods have, and will, come into use. But all of these methods, at their core, are intended to do the same thing—to lead you to this person who has the power, and the desire, to hire you.

Your current circumstances will dictate which job-hunting approach, or approaches, are likely to be most effective for you. And it makes sense to know which approaches are likely to work best under what conditions, so you can spend your job-hunting time as efficiently and productively as possible. With that in mind, let's take a quick look at the various job-hunting methods in use these days and how effective each of these tends to be.

1) Place your resume on an Internet job board, and then sit back and wait for the phone to ring. This is what most people think of when the subject of "job-hunting online" is mentioned. Technology to the rescue!

It's so simple and effective . . . it's enough to make you believe you'll have a job tomorrow.

If you try this approach, you will no doubt discover what just about everyone else who tried it has discovered: this is probably the worst possible use of the Internet for your job-hunt. In fact, it's just about the worst job-hunting method we've come up with so far. Most job boards have up to 40 times as many resumes as job listings. Statistically, the average success rate of this job-hunting method is 4%, or less.

2) Check the job boards for job listings you can apply for. This approach goes hand in hand with the method above. When Internet job-hunting was new, the websites where job-hunters posted resumes were usually separate from the sites where employers posted openings. Combining

PEOPLE WHO NEED PEOPLE

I'm going to keep harping on this throughout the book: job-hunting is all about people. The employer isn't just looking for, say, a Director of Marketing. The employer is looking for a *person* who has the proper skills, temperament, personality, and (you can count on it) looks to operate successfully as Director of Marketing in his company.

And you, the job-hunter, are looking for a *person* who has the power to hire you, who will be likeable to work for, who will give you the chance to prove yourself while you learn the procedures and quirks of that company and the people who work there. If a company is rigidly hierarchical and corporate, it will tend to attract people who are comfortable in that environment. Will you like those people and fit in well with them? Or if you like a lot of structure at work, will you deal well with a company culture

that is a bit more free-spirited? You need to keep this stuff in mind during your job-hunt.

Years ago, when I was writing earlier editions of this book, my editors were constantly correcting me because when I would talk about a website, my tendency is to refer to such a website as "they." Yes, it's improper English, but coming from a programming background, it's firmly fixed in my mind that a website isn't really an "it"—a website is a work product created with an intention, a goal. It is a reflection of what programmers (i.e., people) have created under the direction of one or more managers who want to present certain information to people who visit that website. So whether website or company, you can refer to it as an "it," but your mind needs to remember that it's really him, her, they, them, and those guys.

them into one site was considered kind of visionary at the time. Now, it is extremely rare to find it done any other way.

But whether you post a resume on a job board or go looking for openings there, the success rate is still quite poor. Some job boards are better than others, but in general, most job postings there are not going to help you, unless you take a different approach (listed in method nine). Since it usually costs employers some serious coin to list on most job boards, employers will only put their job listings here when they are unable to fill a position using less expensive approaches. Maybe the position requires a high degree of experience or extensive education in a niche field, or maybe the job is such a drudge that everyone quits after the first month. Or maybe it's a great job . . . but you have to live in a hut just outside the Arctic Circle. When a job is that hard to fill, the odds of you being the right person for it are pretty slim.

So forget what you might have heard; this is not an easy or effective way to find work. In fact, for most people, the success rate for this method is between 4% and 10%. That means that for every 100 people that use this method for their job-hunt (and only this method), between 90 and 96 people will fail; they will *never* find a job.

It is telling that the job boards themselves do not generally release success rates; they would rather talk about their many thousands of visitors per day (the vast majority of whom leave these websites without jobs). And I find it interesting that as late as 2010, Monster had an article posted on their site, detailing how a recent survey showed that one in four people who used Monster received a job offer. The article was dated March of 1998.

Many employers know about the shortcomings of the job boards, and are turning toward posting job openings on their own company websites. This trend, if it continues, means that the job boards will become even less effective than they are now.

3) Send out your resume to various companies; wait for a response. This was actually a popular (and for some people fairly successful) method in the period following World War II. As trades turned into professions, this is what professionals were supposed to do. Its purpose was to generate an invitation for an interview. Once at the interview—where you would be talking with a *person,* face to face—you could dazzle and bewitch with your amazing suitability for the position in question.

Well, it's a numbers game, really, and nowadays, the number that matters most is 7—meaning on average, this job-hunting method has a 7% success rate. In tight times, more people are out of work and fewer positions are available; the numbers are against you. It's common to hear of a thousand resumes sent out with not a single interview resulting. You may remember how many aerospace engineers were flipping burgers at the end of the Apollo space program.

In the last decade, this method has morphed into the "unsolicited email resume," which is treated almost universally by the receiving companies as spam and deleted without a glance. Success rate, done this way, is just about zero.

4) Pay a search firm to find you a job. They go by various names—"Executive Recruiters" and "Executive Placement" are both popular, and have a nice kind of ring, don't you think?—but grand names do not guarantee grand results. The success rate of this approach is between 5% and 24%. The "5%" figure I kind of believe; the "24%" figure I do not. And a further "gotcha" is that the 24% figure applies to jobs with lower salary ranges. If you need to make serious money, the success rate is closer to 5%, or less.

When a job-hunter goes to one of these companies, it's usually because he thinks he is going to a professional, like a doctor or lawyer. Maybe our job-hunter is feeling a little desperate. "Since I need a job," (he thinks), "why not go to the guys who do it every day? The ones who know all the right people? Someone with some *real* ju-ju?"

More often than not, the Executive Placement guy is just a resume writer who wanted to expand his business. He and his employees (if any) usually don't know anyone special, they don't have any more ju-ju than yu-du, and most of the time, they'll just send out resumes for you and cash your checks. And of course they'll be happy to write you a new resume, and cash that check, too.

5) Go to the unemployment office. The success rate of this method is about 14%, on average. Of course, it's not called the "unemployment office" anymore; it will be named "Employment Development Department," or "Department of Employment Security," or something like that. But regardless of the name, if you have been laid off you have no doubt dealt with them already to register for your unemployment check.

As far as the job listings you'll find there, they tend to be low-wage and low-responsibility positions, though there are exceptions. For example, many state, local, and municipal government jobs (including positions in school districts and park and recreation entities) are required by statute to be listed with the local Employment Development office. And if you are receiving any kind of aid (food stamps, AFDC, and so on), you are likely required to be registered there, and at some point may be required to take a job from there, even if you are vastly overqualified or poorly matched in general. But even a bad match (and likely a temporary one) is a job found and helps to boost the success rate of this approach up to that 14% number.

6) Ask everyone you know if they are aware of any job openings, anywhere. This is the simplest form of what is referred to as networking. It is one of the oldest approaches to job-hunting, and even in this crude form, it has a present-day success rate of about 33%. That's not bad. And not only are there ways to improve the success rate, but the Internet is also pretty good at this. Networking, done properly and whole-heartedly, is often said to have a success rate of 60% or higher. More on networking a bit later in the book.

THE UNEMPLOYMENT OFFICE

If you have been terminated from your job, through no fault of your own, it doesn't matter how much you have in the bank right now, you need to *run* to the Employment Development Department (or whatever it is called in your state) and register for your unemployment benefits. There is no shame here; it is your money, you deserve it, and it is there *exactly* for this purpose. You may not be feeling pinched right now, but you have no idea how long it will take to find work, and there may come a time when every nickel is a blessing. Some states allow you to register online, without actually going to the office and standing in line.

Of course, these agencies also have some job listings. They tend to be low-wage and low responsibility positions, but exceptions exist. For example, many state, local, and municipal government jobs (including those in school districts,

and park & recreation entities) are required by statute to be listed with the local Unemployment Office. As long as this is not the sum total of your job-hunting efforts, go ahead and check it out.

Unemployment Offices in the 50 States
www.job-hunt.org/state_unemployment_offices.shtml
This page on Susan Joyce's excellent Gateway site lists state employment offices for all 50 states, as well as links to other job-hunting resources, organized by state.

About.com—Unemployment
http://jobsearch.about.com/od/unemployment/a/unemploymentoff.htm
Another list of the employment offices in the 50 states, and some general information about applying for unemployment benefits.

7) Knock on the door of any place you can think of, and ask if there are any job openings there. This *is* the oldest form of job-hunting, and in the present day, it has a 47% success rate. If the previous approach is "ask everyone you know," then this approach is "ask everyone you don't know." Since there are a lot more people that you don't know, compared to the ones you do, then I guess it makes sense that this approach would have a higher success rate . . . mitigated by your lack of suitability for many of the jobs thus revealed. But when the money's all gone and baby needs shoes. . . .

8) Use the phone book Yellow Pages to identify companies that interest you. Call them and inquire about job openings. Start by using the index to identify industries and fields that interest you, and the listings to identify possible companies in those fields. Pretty much the same as the preceding method, refined somewhat by using the phone book as a research tool, and given a little boost from telephone technology. This approach has a success rate of about 69%.

It should be obvious that this job-hunting method, and the one preceding it, are less geared for the corporate CEO than for the CEO's secretary. If you want to be the head of General Motors, you might consider a different route.

9) Use the Internet to identify industries and fields that interest you; identify companies in your area that are involved in those fields and industries; research these companies thoroughly to see which ones you like best and which will benefit the most from your skills; identify and contact the person with the power to hire in each of these companies.

Along the same lines, use the job boards to see who is hiring. Research those companies. Find out who has the power to hire for positions that interest you, and use research and networking to bypass all those who also saw the listing, but are just sending in resumes.

If the job-hunt benefited from advances in available technology when the telephone came along, then the Internet is even better, by orders of magnitude. And really, research is what the Internet is best at. There is a huge amount of information at your fingertips—more every day—and all you have to do is learn how to find it. This is what much of this book is about.

What is the success rate of this approach? I don't know. It's too new. My guess would be somewhere around 75%, but variations in how people go about this (and how hard they actually work at it) no doubt make the method more effective for some people than others.

10) Perform the kind of self-assessment and targeted job-hunt described in *What Color Is Your Parachute?* This approach to finding a job was originally created in the 1960s and 70s by pioneers in the career field who saw how poorly other job-hunting methods were working. For the past forty years, *What Color Is Your Parachute?* has been updated yearly and is the most popular job-hunting book of all time, period. It's no mystery why this is so; the method detailed in *Parachute* has an 86% success rate.

There isn't room here to do anything more than give you a general outline of what is often referred to as *the Parachute process,* but at its essence, it revolves around What, Where, and How:

What are the skills that you most enjoy using? Once identified, and knowing that your skills are transferable from one job, field, and industry to another, you will want to identify:

Where you want to use these skills. Are there certain fields that attract you? Do you have special knowledge, trade familiarity, or industry expertise that draws you to certain fields? And once such fields are identified, what sort of company do you want to work at? Large? Small? Do you want a company dominant in its market, or would you prefer the open horizons in a startup? The clearer the picture you can draw for yourself about the type of place you want to work, the easier it will be to determine:

How you will go about the specifics of your job-hunt: identifying and targeting the organizations that interest you, in the fields which most attract you. In researching these organizations, you will identify what their needs are, how your skills would be useful to them, who in the organization has the power to hire you, and how best to approach that person and show how you can benefit the organization.

Okay, now you know ten of the most common job-hunting methods currently in use and their average success rates. Which method is going to work best for you? The simple answer is I don't know, and you don't either, at least not yet. No method is perfect, some methods work better for certain people, or certain companies, or certain industries . . . and this list doesn't include every possible approach to job-hunting.

Moreover, there's nothing that says you can only use one job-hunting method. In fact, the experts say that you are more likely to find a job if you are using more than one method, although this advice contains a gotcha: multiple methods work great as long as you don't use more than three different methods at the same time. If you are using more than three different approaches, they all tend to become (statistically speaking) less successful.

As you go through your job-hunt, it will soon become apparent which approach, or approaches, or combination of approaches, are or are not working for you; and none of this stuff is written in stone. If you decide that you should call some places, visit others, send some a resume . . . the object is to get the best job in the least amount of time. If that doesn't happen, what does it matter that you're doing all of the dance steps properly?

While looking at the different approaches to job-hunting, one thing will become quite clear: there is a direct correlation with how hard you work at your job-hunt, and how good the job is that you end up with. If you want the highest salary, the best work environment, and the greatest work satisfaction, then you have to work harder to find that job. We've all known people who, regardless of what they are doing, always seem to be looking for the shortcut. That's why the less desirable jobs are usually saved for the less desirable employees.

JOB-HUNT SUCCESS RATES

When you look at the success rates for the different job-hunting methods, remember that these are just statistics. You have only to listen to a political debate to know that numbers and statistics are great when you're marshalling an argument, but that's really all these statistics are: an argument. The success rates I have given show the average experiences of average people. By listing these success rates, I am making the argument that these same experiences will probably apply to you . . . but we shouldn't confuse an argument with an answer. Naturally, don't ignore the experiences of those who have gone before you; that would be foolish. But everyone *is* different, and who knows? You may be seriously non-average.

You can also look at the success rates and take a completely different approach. If a job-hunting method has a statistical effectiveness of 10%, that doesn't mean you shouldn't try it; just don't spend more than 10% of your job-hunting time using it. String together two or three different methods, and soon you can be using more than 100% of your job-hunting time effectively.

And probably the most important thing to remember is that if a job-hunting method secures you the job you want, then it doesn't matter what the averages are for other job-hunters. For you, that method is 100% successful.

Keeping Up with Change

As the list of job-hunting methods demonstrates, the way that people approach the job-hunt has changed over time. What new trends may affect the job-hunt by the time you read this? Since the nature of book publishing does not allow for quick updates, we'll have to turn to the Internet to learn about what changes may be affecting the job-hunting world.

The Job-Hunting Online Website
http://job-huntingonline.webs.com/
This is the official support website for readers of this book. Here you will find any URL changes and corrections, updates, and whatever else might be useful to readers as time passes. There may also be articles and links to various resources that you may find helpful.

Job-Hunter's Bible
www.jobhuntersbible.com/
The official website for *What Color Is Your Parachute?*, every job-hunter should have a recent copy of this book on their bookshelf. The website has helpful information for job-hunters, including how to sign up for seminars with author and career-search expert Richard Bolles.

Job-Hunting: Online Guides

The web has a number of guides to job-hunting, freely accessible, usually helpful. They will not all agree with each other on all subjects, but the websites listed here contain job-hunting guides that are, generally speaking, well-informed, helpful, and well-maintained—that is, the information on these sites is well tended and updated at reasonable intervals.

Job Search Manual
www.sunraye.com/job_net/index.html
A fairly comprehensive guide, though not a great amount of information about using the Internet in your job hunt; and a bit dated in some other respects. Still, a good resource to have, and you can't beat the price (since it's free). As with all job-hunting information, take the good and leave the rest.

Finding a Job
www.bc.edu/offices/careers/jobs.html
From the Boston College website, an excellent resource.

The Online Job Search Tutorial
www.job-hunt.org/starting.shtml
From Susan Joyce's Job-Hunt.org site, a very complete three-part tutorial.

College Grad Job-Hunter
www.collegegrad.com/jobsearch/Intro/
Author Brian Krueger's book, *College Grad Job Hunter,* (Adams Media, 2008), available in bookstores, is also available online. For free. The book is aimed at the college graduate, emphasizing techniques to use when you have academic knowledge but not much real-world experience. He also points out that job-hunting is an experience that you should start preparing for before it happens, and there is a lot of good advice for all job-hunters. I think that some of his guerilla tactics should be avoided, but this is a minor complaint; it's a great online resource.

The Job-Employment Guide
www.job-employment-guide.com/
A pretty decent guide, with sections on career planning and assessment, resumes and cover letters, job search, interviews and salary negotiations, and even some information about self-employment. Like many websites of this sort, there is not as much depth as we might like.

And Try These Search Terms
If the listings above aren't helpful in your situation, or you want to look at other sites, try plugging the following terms into a search engine:

job hunting guide	*job hunting manual*
job hunting eguide	*job search guide*
job search manual	*job search tips*

Job-Hunting: Online Articles

The web is brimming with articles about job-hunting. As time passes, it's becoming more difficult to find the ones that burn brightest in a field that always tends to generate more heat than light. The ones I have listed here are all good, for various reasons. There will be more links to articles about Internet research, contacts, resumes, job boards, and so forth as we proceed through the book.

The Info Pro's Survival Guide to Job-hunting
www.infotoday.com/searcher/jul02/mort.htm
If you only read one article for your job-hunt, this should be the one. Although written for librarians and information professionals, and possibly a bit advanced for some readers at this stage of the game, author Mary-Ellen Mort makes some interesting points about why traditional job-hunting techniques are so ineffective. She gives a number of tips on finding the Hidden Job Market, and a sidebar explains why job boards, from Monster and CareerBuilder down to the smallest regionals, are not as successful as we might wish.

The Dirty Dozen Online Job-Hunting Mistakes
www.job-hunt.org/jobsearchmistakes.shtml
An excellent article from one of the best Gateway job sites.

10 Job-Hunting Tips from People Who Found Jobs
www.forbes.com/2010/06/23/job-seeking-advice-leadership-careers-hiring.html
A good article from Forbes; hits the high points.

Forum—Ask the Hiring Manager
www.collegegrad.com/forum/all.shtml
From the CollegeGrad.com website, this is a series of questions and answers on a variety of subjects related to job-hunting. As mentioned above, the CollegeGrad site is aimed at students and recent college graduates, who generally lack experience at the job-hunt game. But the site has a lot to offer everyone, recent college graduate or not.

And Try These Search Terms
job hunting advice   *job hunting articles*
job hunting sites   *job hunting mistakes*
career articles   *career sites*
job search advice   *job search tips*

Gateways

Okay, now that you are armed with a little bit of information and have decided that *now* is the time to go job-hunting, there are a number of first steps you should take. For the most part, these steps are each, by themselves, pretty easy to do; no really hard work or great expenditures of time.

Probably the best place to start online is at the sites where you will find the largest amount of useful information in the least amount of time. These are the Gateway sites I mentioned in chapter 1.

Gateways are starting places, doorways to the net, organized to give you both an overview of the job-hunt as well as specific resources that will help you as you perform your own. So rather than punching "job hunting" into a search engine and then having to deal with the 33 million (Google), 54 million (Yahoo/Bing), or 218 million (yikes . . . Quintura) results that are returned, you can instead go to the Gateway sites, secure in the knowledge that people who know what they are doing have already done the searching, sifting, organizing, and evaluating.

SEARCH ENGINE RELEVANCE

How does a search engine decide what gets put at the top of the list of search results? (The industry calls this "ordering by relevance.") Techniques vary, but most search engines base their rankings on data instances and page links. How many times does your search term come up in the search engine's database—more on some pages than others? And how many other web pages link to this one? The theory being that if a lot of other web pages mention the content of, or link to, a certain site, then the data there has the ring of authority.

But it's a purely automatic process, and the technique has weaknesses.

Relevance can change due to bursts of interest from the online community or by artificial means that mimic such interest. Linking itself can be manipulated; knowing how the search engines rank results makes it possible to skew the ranking of the data that a search engine returns.

Why is this important? Think about it the next time you only look at the first page of search results. And if you need more clues, think about why the Supersites come up when you Google "job search engines."

The best Gateways are well-organized information clearing-houses. They have articles about various aspects of the job-hunt, where you can learn more about the *process* of job-hunting, and how to go about it effectively. There are links to other sites on the web where you can get more specific information, relevant to your particular job-hunt. Since the links you will find at these Gateways have all been vetted by knowledgeable people, you will save huge amounts of time and energy by going to them first, rather than trying to sift through the avalanche of information that general search engines provide. Open the door and step on through; many paths and possibilities will be laid out in front of you.

The Gateway sites listed here are all stable, mature websites, run by people that are considered authorities in the career and job-hunting fields. This is not to say that they are all equally knowledgeable, or will give all tactics the same weight, or will all give the same advice in all circumstances. But as you explore these sites—as with any authority—you should have good reasons to ignore the advice given.

Gateway sites are not perfect. As with all things Internet, they are a mix of good and bad. And as time passes, I find that some of the Gateway sites are not all that they once were, and tend to suffer from the same flaws. These flaws are not fatal, but they are there none the less, and you should be aware of them, to wit:

- The articles tend to be drawn with broad strokes rather than detailed ones. There is a growing trend toward brief articles that lack depth and nuance (an Internet-wide trait). You must read more articles to gain the same insights that you used to find in a single page. This wouldn't be so important if it didn't steal the job-hunter's most precious commodity, and one that cannot be replaced: time.

- As with most sites throughout the web, there is an increasing move to monetize Gateway websites. This might sound like a picayune, whiney complaint . . . why shouldn't website owners make money from their efforts? It's a matter of balance, I guess. There are Gateway sites that I was pleased to include in past editions of this book that I no longer list, principally because of this issue. Why does this matter? Again, as you try to navigate through various boxes, pay-per-click hotspots, and advertisements on a web page, your time is being stolen as you try to divine if a resource is presented because it benefits the job-hunter, or because it benefits the owner of the website. Often, it's both . . . but how much of each? Where does the tipping point lie? It's hard to serve two masters.

In spite of these flaws though, Gateways are *hugely* helpful to the job-hunter and are updated regularly. Often, new trends and tactics will be described at the Gateways first.

CareerOneStop

www.careeronestop.org

Sponsored by the US Department of Labor, CareerOneStop has a huge amount of data for the job-hunter. Information on unemployment benefits, career centers, career changing, retraining, employer research, licensing and certification . . . there's far too much to list, but if you can imagine it, it's probably here. No advertising to clutter the site, just (a sometimes bewildering amount of) information.

Job-hunt

www.job hunt.org

One of the best Gateways, from one of our best authorities, Susan Joyce. Here you will find a wealth of information on job-hunting and using the Internet effectively, current articles about the world of work, and many links to job-search resources and industry journals. If you have a question about some aspect of the job-hunt, this site is one of the first places you should go.

One of the fields that Susan is particularly skilled in is how to create an Internet presence for yourself during your job-hunt by using social-network sites (Facebook, Twitter, LinkedIn, and the like).

The Riley Guide

www.rileyguide.com

Run by Margaret Riley Dikel, the Riley Guide is an excellent site for job-hunters. Margaret knows her subject, and the articles she writes for her site tend to have more depth and insight than the norm.

Quintessential Careers

www.quintcareers.com/portal.html

This Gateway has thousands of pages, leading to all kinds of resources. The site, though extremely comprehensive, could use an update to its look and organization—it doesn't fit modern computer screens well; single articles often lack depth, requiring a *lot* of mouse clicking to get to the information you are looking for; and sell-you-something pop-up pages abound. Still, even though it's not the best of the Gateway sites, there is much here that is good.

Job-Hunting Link Pages

The Gateway sites I have listed above are the ones I believe will be the most useful for the greatest number of readers, but if you feel you need further information about job-hunting in general, here are some more sites with helpful information, links to articles, and other resources:

JobStar
http://jobstar.org/jobstar.php
Run by Mary-Ellen Mort, this is a great site . . . but her funding only covers California, so the site is extremely California-centric. Were it not for this, I'd be able to give the site more focus. Still, the many links you'll find here are helpful regardless of where you live; give it a look.

Web Lens
www.weblens.org/career.html
From the wide-ranging mind of Pam Blackstone.

About.com—Career Planning
http://careerplanning.about.com/
http://jobsearch.about.com/
About.com is a wonderful resource; its career section is especially good.

Blogs

For those who don't know, "blog"—easily my least favorite name for anything I can think of at the moment—is a contraction of "web log" or "weblog." It begs the question: where were all of the imaginative, innovative people when it came time to name these things? And "blogosphere" is even worse.

Okay, that's my blog for today, and it beats a lot of the others you'll find out there. The average job-hunting blog is more notable for its firm grasp of the obvious than for any new and innovative approaches to the job search. And yet, blogs are often where new ideas about job-hunting can be found. For this reason alone, you should be familiar with some of the better bloggers around. Here are a few:

Nick Corcodillos—Ask The Headhunter

http://corcodilos.com/blog/

Nick is smart, knowledgeable, and not shy about speaking his mind. One of our best job-hunting bloggers.

Job-Hunt.org—Susan Joyce

www.job-hunt.org/online-job-search-guide.shtml

Though not necessarily a "blogger" per se, Susan writes regularly and keeps past articles on this page.

The Riley Guide—Blog List

www.rileyguide.com/

From the Riley Guide Gateway site, this page has links to a number of job-hunt blogs.

Alison's Job Searching Blog

http://jobsearch.about.com/b/

Also at http://jobsearch.about.com/

Alison is the author of many of the excellent career articles at About.com. Her blogs tend to be bite-size rather than full-course meals; choose whichever you like, according to your appetite.

Penelope Trunk—Brazen Careerist

http://blog.penelopetrunk.com/

Penelope has some ideas that do not enjoy universal acceptance; others are pretty neat. I personally like her irreverent writing style.

100 Best Blogs for Your Job Search

www.jobprofiles.org/library/job-search/100_best_blogs_for_your_job_search.htm

Might be stronger on the quantity than the quality, but at least there's lots to choose from.

Career-Related Blogs for Job-Seekers

www.quintcareers.com/career-related_blogs.html

Links to a number of job-hunting and career-related blogs, from the Quint-Careers site.

The Supersites

Monster, CareerBuilder, and HotJobs: these job boards are the Supersites, the first places that most people think of when you mention online job-hunting. (Monster has bought HotJobs from Yahoo!, so by the time you read this, it's possible that HotJobs may have lost its independent identity, swallowed by Monster.) In addition to their Internet presence, one of the Supersites has probably taken over your newspaper's former want-ad section. Online, their visitors have been measured in the millions; a survey, taken a few years back, showed that 89% of online job-hunters had registered with Monster. Similar figures exist for the other two Supersites.

To understand the popularity of the Supersites, you need to know a little about how online job boards work. At its core, a job board starts with a database. (A database is a collection of similar data records: in this case, job listings and/or resumes.) Now add a search function to check whether words in a job listing match up with the words in a resume. The search function is not very sophisticated; it cannot divine intent. All it does is check whether the proper words (called keywords) match up. Whether you are matching job listings to resumes or resumes to job listings is irrelevant; the task is the same. Now, wrap it in an attractive package—maybe add some articles and other services to look helpful and authoritative to job-hunters—and put it on the web. Bingo, you've got a job board. There are *thousands* of these on the Internet.

With very few exceptions, job boards exist to make money. Most do this by charging employers to post job listings (it's rare for the job-hunter to pay a fee). Naturally, job boards all want employers to list with them, not their competitors. So each board says it is more efficient than the competition; that is, the employers will get a better return on their money, in the form of more and better-suited applicants, than they would if they were to list their jobs on (and give their money to) other job boards. In order to prove that their board is the most efficient, the people that run a particular job board will often use one of two arguments: we are better because we specialize, or we are better because we are bigger.

Employers are no different than anyone else: they want to get the most for their money. So if they decide to go the job board route, they'll have to decide which one they should use.

It makes sense to go where they think the most job-hunters will go; or at least the kind of job-hunters they want to hire. If the employer is in a moderately specialized field—electronics engineering, for example, or maybe health care—they might go to a job board that specializes in that field. For example, Dice is a well-respected job board that specializes in tech jobs, while Absolutely Health Care is a popular job board for careers in medicine. There are thousands of these specialized job boards on the Internet, catering to a wide range of fields and industries.

Another way that a job board might specialize is to limit their job listings to a certain geographical area. Why should you care if a job board has thousands of potential jobs, if none of them are near you, or where you want to live? So many job boards will take listings for all fields and industries, but limit the listings to a certain area; BostonJobs, or Bay Area Help Wanted, are typical.

But specialize schmecialize—to many people, BIG is best.

Imagine, for a moment, that a) all job-hunters and employers use job boards, and b) there is only one job board on the Internet. Everyone goes here, meaning that *all* job-hunters post their resumes here, and it is here that *all* employers place their job openings. If the job you are looking for exists, *this* is where you will find it. If you want to hire someone, and the person you need is alive, on the planet, and in need of work, *this* is where you will find him or her.

Of course, this is not the case; but some job boards would like you to think it is. Thus, the Supersites: job boards that count primarily on their size to convince employers that *this* is the place to post their job listings, because *every* job-hunter comes here. "Why, just look at the millions of visitors we have every month!" And once they have the listings, they can say to the job-hunter, "Hey, we've got more job listings than anyone else, come to our site," which convinces the employers to post more, which brings more job-hunters, and on it goes with each side feeding the other. If you convince enough employers to post their job listings, then you can even afford to buy commercial time during the Super Bowl. You can afford to take over your newspaper's help-wanted section. You can offer to manage the employment areas of many company websites, and even sell pre-packaged Internet job boards.

So the popularity of the Supersites comes pretty much from size alone and the increased visibility that such size confers. All well and good; but we are still left to wonder: why are they so ineffective?

To start with, you should know that posting a job opening with one of the Supersites costs the employer hundreds of dollars for a typical job listing. So the job postings on the Supersites tend to be for jobs that are more difficult for the employer to fill—otherwise, he would happily fill them without spending money. What it boils down to is that many Supersite postings represent jobs that are slightly less desirable, or require higher levels of experience and education. The odds are that much lower that you will meet the requirements the employer is looking for, and, if you do get a job this way, it's less likely that you will be happy with it.

Moreover, not all of the job listings on the Supersites represent real jobs. Historically, Monster and CareerBuilder have accepted job listings from agencies, recruiters, and companies that are looking to sell their wares and services to job-hunters, but whose job listings are really only a way of gathering names and addresses. Also, many companies like to keep their brand out there for people to see, even when they are not actively hiring at the moment. And if that isn't enough, the Supersites are great targets for people who put up false job listings, mining the resumes they get for personal information in order to perpetrate one scam or another.

Of course, such bogus listings are not the Supersites' fault; at least not directly. They can't afford to make sure there is a real job behind every job listing they get, and of course there is the financial pressure to sell more and more job listings.

And finally, in the interests of fairness, I have to tell you that most other job boards—the many thousands of specialty boards, for example—suffer from many of the same flaws, and are not all that much more successful than the Supersites at finding people jobs. Job boards, the way most people use them, are just not the best use of your Internet time.

So if this is such a poor way of job-hunting, why am I taking all this time talking about job boards and the Supersites? The answer is simple: you probably don't believe me. So many people have it in their minds that *this* is what online job-hunting is all about that the only way they will learn otherwise is to give it a try. So: give it a try. Take a look at some of the Supersites. There are a lot of job listings there, and if you are one of the 4% (or whatever) of people that find work this way, then the Supersites' effectiveness is not 4%. If you get a job this way, then for you, their effectiveness is 100%. Can't do better than that.

But this advice comes with some warnings. If the chances of getting a job offer is 4%, let's use that statistic a new way and say that you should not spend more than 4% of your job-hunting time at the Supersites. Go ahead and sign up, look through the job listings, maybe post your resume . . . you never know. If you only spend a few minutes at it and you get a terrific job, then great; sometimes you do strike oil. But just as you shouldn't try to pay the rent by betting on the horses, don't limit yourself to the Supersites as your only job-search strategy.

Also, you might want to read the rest of this book, especially chapter 6, before you post your resume on *any*-site. When posting your resume—or anything else for that matter—you are giving up control of that data. You are, quite literally, giving it away and usually losing control over what is done with it. (If you're short on nightmares lately, read the Terms of Use for the job boards and Supersites.)

Moreover, if you post your resume today, it becomes part of your overall Internet persona. A few weeks down the road, you may find that you should have written it differently; too bad, too late. Your first resume might be passed on to employers, recruiters, and so forth, taking on an Internet life of its own. If you then post a different resume later, you can easily end up with conflicting data about yourself making the rounds. Some employers don't like this, and it is becoming common for employers to do a little online research about people they are thinking about hiring. Conflicting data can hurt you, especially if something you posted is sort of like, um, not true? Wow, bummer.

Monster
www.monster.com

HotJobs
http://hotjobs.yahoo.com

CareerBuilder
www.careerbuilder.com

The Job Search Engines

Search engines are what make using the Internet possible. There is so much data available, spread over such a vast area without rhyme or reason, that without search engine technology, the Internet would be practically useless.

We'll look more closely at search engines in chapter 6, but for now, you should know that a search engine consists of a crawler, or spider, that roams the net (or specific places on the net) and builds a database, or index, about what it finds. When you enter a search term, the search engine looks at its index, and if it finds a match to your inquiry, it tells you where it found that data.

You are probably used to working with one of the general information search engines such as Google, Yahoo!, and so on. But there are specialized search engines, too. For example, instead of looking for an encyclopedic range of data, what if you told the spider to only look for job listings?

Well, like every other good idea I've ever had, someone else already thought of this. For some years now, there have been job search engines available on the web. Some of these job search engines search company websites, building an index of the job listings found there. Others don't actually go out and search the web; instead, they accept data feeds from certain job boards, and build their index from these feeds. Though similar to job search engines, and commonly called search engines, sites that operate this way are technically known as aggregators. Many job aggregators also accept job listings from employers, just as a regular job board would.

Again, technology has come to the rescue. Now you don't have to go, one by one, to all of the Supersites, career pages, and other job boards scattered around the web; the job search engines and aggregators will do it for you.

Or will they? Though most job search engines and aggregators will indicate where each of its job listings came from, you don't always know which job boards and career sites are included, or are only partially included. Furthermore, the technology cannot tell which of the job listings are real; all of the undesirable jobs, phishing scams, recruiter lead-building, and other misleading posts that exist on the job boards become part of the database. And finally, most have no way of weeding out duplicate job listings, so you shouldn't pay too much attention to how many jobs they claim to have in the database.

But still—these job search engines and aggregators have a very wide reach, and are so easy to use, it seems silly to not give them a try. Just bear in mind all of the caveats about job boards, the Supersites, and 4%.

Let's start with the aggregators:

SimplyHired

www.simplyhired.com

SimplyHired is probably the best of the aggregators, with a nice interface. Their database is culled from "job boards, company pages, online classifieds and other data sources." You can search or browse the listings, by geographical area, job title, field, and industry.

SimplyHired offers trend data, showing you graphs of various aspects of the employment market; I'm not sure how helpful that is, but the charts are pretty.

Probably less pretty, but certainly more helpful, is the fact that SimplyHired is meshed with LinkedIn, the well-known business networking site. When a job listing pops up at a certain company, you can find out with the press of a button if your LinkedIn network includes anyone at that company.

Like most aggregators, SimplyHired encourages employers to feed them their job listings, as well as pay for sponsored listings. Furthermore, if you want to put a job board on your website, SimplyHired will sell you one, complete with job listings. Bear *that* in mind as you click around the web, visiting various job boards, thinking they are all unique and individual.

Indeed

www.indeed.com/

Indeed is one of the more popular job aggregators. Their job listings come from (to quote the site) "major job boards, newspapers, associations and company career pages," giving you a large database of job listings to look through. It also allows you to browse through job listings by state and by industry field. You get access to salary and job trends in various fields, and forums dealing with various fields and jobs. The site allows you to download plug-ins that integrate Indeed's job-search functions into your web browser, and you can be alerted by email whenever a new job in

GOOGLE BOMBING

Taken to extremes, the skewing of search results' relevance is sometimes known as "Google bombing." The first wide-spread example of Google bombing I know of came soon after the 2003 American invasion of Iraq. A Google search for the term "weapons of mass destruction" brought up a realistic-looking Google-style error page, saying that no such weapons can be displayed (you can view it at www.coxar.pwp.blueyonder.co.uk/). Following that, some people got together and caused the query phrase "miserable failure" to return President Bush's biography from the White House website. And of course Bush supporters then Google bombed Hillary Clinton, Michael Moore, and others.

What does this have to do with job-hunting? I have no idea.

your field of interest comes in. Moreover, you can read success stories from people who found jobs through Indeed on their forum.

If a listing does not contain salary data, Indeed "estimates" what the salary is. This is really nothing more than a computer looking at salary trends for similar positions and making a WAG, which stands for "wild guess" after editing. This is not a practice I expect the site to continue for too long, so it may be gone by the time you read this.

Indeed also accepts paid job listings directly from employers on a pay-per-click basis. This is a bit unfortunate, as it inevitably leads to even more bogus job postings from recruiters, agencies, and companies that sell services to job-hunters. But at least these "sponsored jobs" are well defined, just as a search engine's sponsored results are. Like everything on the Internet (and in life), perfection is elusive.

Beyond Aggregating

Linkup
www.linkup.com

Two trends are changing the online job-hunting landscape. The first is that almost every company you can think of has its own website. The second is that many companies are looking for alternatives to the job boards, and are turning toward using their own websites to post their job openings.

Enter Linkup. Linkup is more of a job search engine than an aggregator. It does not send its spider to the Supersites—or any job board, for that matter. Instead, it takes advantage of the trend toward employer self-sufficiency in the hiring arena and looks at the postings on employer websites to build its database. This gives a much purer database; the problematic job listings commonly found on the job boards are eliminated. Linkup has also chosen not to index jobs from "headhunters, search firms, staffing companies, temporary staffing firms, and independent recruiters." Though it can be argued that this eliminates many good potential jobs, I can see their point—it also eliminates many of the problems with bogus listings, resume collecting, and duplicate positions. As I write, their spider visits about twenty-two thousand corporate websites daily, resulting in around half a million current jobs in the database; they plan to have forty thousand companies by the time you read this, with an eventual target of around one hundred thousand, a figure they believe to be effectively equal to "all useful corporate websites."

Linkup does allow employers to advertise jobs using the same pay-per-click approach that is so common on the web nowadays, but does not allow employers to automatically post jobs into their database using XML feeds (don't worry about it, your life will be no better for knowing). Again, less garbage in the database.

Job aggregators and search engines are still working out the bugs and finding their place in the job-hunting landscape; as such, they are a bit of a moving target. Yet I think that this can be a useful approach to your job-hunt. Not the only approach, of course; we are still talking about first steps for you to take. But this is a step and not a stumble. Spend a little time at these sites and see if something turns up.

However—jumping around to many different job search engines is not a worthwhile way to spend your time. I've listed the best ones, and although it's possible that the future will bring stunning new advances in the technology that will make the ones listed above totally obsolete, that's not likely.

Also, search engines can be "massaged." There are companies whose only business is to make sure *your* company website is listed at the top of the results pages in the common search engines; they call this "search engine optimization," because that sounds better than "gaming the system." (See Search Engine Relevance sidebar on page 23.) This explains why, when you ask Google to search on the term "job search engines," the first results page includes CareerBuilder, Monster, and HotJobs. None of which are job search engines.

craigslist

www.craigslist.org

You live in a community; in an online sense, craigslist is a pretty good reflection of it. Tremendously successful, craigslist is local, simple, and in almost all cases, free. Since the death of the newspaper want ad (see Newspaper Classified sidebar on page 36), it is to craigslist that many local employers now turn when they want to post a job listing. And since posting on craigslist costs employers less than the job boards, that makes this site a good resource for the job-hunter. You won't see many corporate CEO jobs listed here, but that's okay. As long as you aren't looking for a specialized or extremely high-salary position, it's a good idea to spend ten minutes or so each morning taking a look at what is available in the craigslist "jobs" section. (You'll notice that craigslist does not believe in capital letters.)

Clicking on "jobs" allows you to see *all* job postings, regardless of category. They are only organized by the order in which they were added to the site. Or, you can click on the (somewhat generalized) job-category headings and see only the job listings in a particular category.

But even beyond that, there are two ways to look through the job listings on craigslist. One way is to *browse*—that is, to read through (or at least skim) each listing, one at a time, and the other is to *search,* using craigslist's search function. Browsing takes more time, but it's unlikely that you'll miss a listing that uses an unexpected job title or description. Searching is fast, but it requires you to think of the correct job title or description. What do you do if the employer uses a different job title, or describes it in a (to you) unusual way? If you don't put the right words in the search box, you'll never see it. Someone else will get that job.

Well, you don't have the time to browse *every* job in the "jobs" section—craigslist gets a *lot* of job postings. Instead, *browse* the listings under the job headings that seem likely, and then *search* the whole "jobs" area for probable job titles. The job you are perfectly suited for may be listed under a job title that you would never think of, or a category that seems odd. So the "browse some, search all" approach, though not foolproof, works pretty well. Job listings are organized by date posted, so it's easy to just check in and see what has been added since your last visit.

There is a craigslist for every major city in the United States. Most minor ones have one, too. California has almost thirty, New York state has twenty,

NEWSPAPER CLASSIFIEDS

The newspaper want-ad, as we have known it for many years, is effectively dead. Once considered a critical source of newspaper revenue (and the first place most people looked when job-hunting), most newspapers now farm out this feature, primarily to companies associated with the Supersites. In fact, CareerBuilder is owned by newspaper companies Tribune and Gannett. Monster bought HotJobs in 2010, in part, to increase its reach into the newspaper-classified contracts that HotJobs holds. This makes looking at newspaper classifieds a waste of time; such job listings are just taken from listings on the Supersite that holds that newspaper's contract. If going the classifieds route, most local employers (particularly the smaller ones) now post their job openings with craigslist.

and on it goes. Each city's craigslist site has a completely separate job section, with its own listings, so you can scout nearby cities and towns for jobs, as well as plan for moving cross country. Or farther: craigslist presently has hundreds of sites in more than seventy countries.

Another useful section on craigslist is "gigs." The jobs listed can be temporary, one-time, or project-based jobs. When you are running low on money and the job-hunt is taking a long time, "gigs" is a great place to pick up some short-term work. Moreover, the people who post here might know where you can find full-time employment, or be able to provide leads to others who do. And like temporary and volunteer work, it is not unusual for a gig, performed well by you, to expand into a regular job.

There is also a "resumes" section, where you can post your resume for free. If you decide to post there, don't post your whole resume. There has been too much hanky panky on craigslist over the years for you to drop your guard and post a lot of data about yourself. Instead, post a resume as described in chapter 4, or use this area to write a "job wanted" kind of listing, with your basic qualifications and experience. You don't even have to give out your email address; people can contact you through craigslist. If you get a legitimate response, then you can proceed to normal communication without fear of being victimized.

And of course, if you need to generate a little cash by selling your old stair-stepper, or are looking for a roommate to help with the rent, craigslist allows you to do that kind of stuff, too.

And Don't Forget . . .

This would be a good time to box up your TV's remote control, and send it to yourself, book rate. (Don't worry, it'll be back in a few weeks.) Better yet, cancel all of your premium services—HBO, Showtime, sports channels, and so on—and just leave yourself with the most basic channels. You can still watch the evening news (though a newspaper would be better), and if there's something you really need to watch, you can sit down to watch that specific program. Liberated from your remote, you won't be doing much channel surfing, unless you like getting up from the couch about a hundred times an hour.

And here's why: the *Wall Street Journal*'s Economics Editor has cited surveys that show that the unemployed in the United States spend, on average, forty minutes every day job-hunting, and two-hundred minutes watching TV. This is one of those little factoids that's painful to contemplate from any number of angles: over three hours of television every day, when you need to be looking for a job? Five times as much TV watching, compared to working your job-hunt? A half hour of commercials pouring into your brain every day?

You need to make job-hunting your job. Eight hours a day. The job-hunt is too important for you to approach it with anything less than passion and commitment . . . characteristics that your next employer might like to see you demonstrate, by the way.

Remember that you are in a competition with all of the other job-hunters out there. If the average job-hunt takes thirty weeks, and the average job-hunter spends more time watching TV than working his job-hunt, then you need to be *above* average. While your competitors are watching sitcoms, you can be beating them out of a job. While the next guy spends a few hours a day job-hunting, you can spend eight or ten hours a day. Who do you think is going to get hired first, at the better position, with the best salary? If you want the best job, you have to be the hardest working job-hunter. It's that simple.

By the way, any teenagers in the house may complain about the loss of the TV. Just explain to them the concept of a "book." Maybe show them some examples.

Chapter 3

SKILLS

BEFORE WE DEAL WITH RESUMES in chapter 4, we need to talk a bit about skills. You can think of a resume as a diagram of the skills you possess and want to use in your next job. And when an employer reads your resume, he should be able to very quickly see that you have the skills he is looking for. Obviously, in order for your resume to tell him this much, you need to have a clear idea of what your skills are.

You could argue that there are situations where such knowledge is unnecessary. For example, say you are applying for a position as a legal secretary. You've been a legal secretary for the last twenty years, why do you need to break down the job title into composite skills? The skills involved are inherent in the job title. But what if you are having trouble finding legal secretary positions? Most people change careers at least three times in their working life, and skills are transferable from one job to another, from one industry to another. If legal secretary jobs are hard to come by, you can examine the skills you have used as a legal secretary and see what other jobs use a similar skill set. This way, you open up more possibilities for yourself.

Knowing your skills and being able to cast them in the proper light are important not only if you are planning to change careers but also if you are young and lack work experience, or if you have large gaps in your employment history.

But what happens if you need to change careers, yet you have no clear idea of what your skills really are? And, what do you do if you hate what you have been doing, but don't know what you *want* to do? Maybe there are some tests you could take?

The point of any test, exercise, or instrument is to find out more about *you*. What engages you? What do you care about? What do you enjoy doing with your time when you are *not* working? If you want to be happy in your work, there's no point in looking for a job that requires skills you don't enjoy using, in a working environment you find barely tolerable, making things or otherwise obtaining results you have no interest in. And face it: many of us still have it stuck somewhere in the back of our minds that "work" is what we don't especially like doing, and "recreation" (or whatever term you like for "not work") is when we're enjoying ourselves.

So the first thing to do is take a look at what you like, what you enjoy, what excites you. Wouldn't it be great if your next job is one where your alarm clock goes off and you don't want to keep hitting the snooze button?

To this end, there are a number of online assessments or instruments that can help you focus on what you would be happiest doing. These fall into three basic categories:

- Personality
- Career Interests and Values
- Skills

Note that most of the personality and career interest tests that are much beloved by many career counselors are *not* available online without charge; and just because they have a price tag doesn't mean they are worth money. Start with the free versions; if they don't tell you what you want to know, consider the possibility that no test of that sort—regardless of cost—is going to give you the answers you seek.

I would caution you to be careful how much weight you give *any* test. People are complex, contradictory, frustrating creatures that defy easy classification, and none of us fit in a neat, easily defined box. The results of any of these tests are to be considered as a kind of loose guideline, a trail to explore. If the results of a test feel wrong to you, listen to your feelings.

Online Testing: Personality

When you go online, the most widely available career-oriented tests are personality inventories. Of these, the two most common are versions of the Meyers-Briggs Type Indicator, often referred to as the MBTI, and to a lesser extent, the Enneagram. The theory behind using these types of tests is that a person's personality should match—or at least not conflict—with the tasks necessary in certain occupations. Someone who craves human contact will hate being shut up alone in a small office; someone with a quiet personality, who avoids conflict at all costs, will make a poor supervisor . . . like that. In situations such as these, one could certainly argue that "personality" is not without career *implications,* at the very least.

I am not convinced that online personality tests, as they are currently implemented, are all that helpful to most job-hunters. Often, one will see job titles or potential careers linked to the test results, but the range of careers suggested is so wide and varied as to be effectively useless. High school students may find such tests somewhat beneficial for hinting at several general career directions, but for working adults, these types of tests are better at illuminating the *style* with which you might perform a job, than actually predicting what career that style implies. It takes far more than style to define a job or career. Therefore, look at all personality-based career suggestions with a skeptical eye, and consider spending your time with more effective routes to truth.

Having said that, if you believe that these personality tests will be helpful in your job-hunt, then go ahead and give them a try. You'll notice that there are no free online versions of the *full* Meyers-Briggs or Enneagram instruments. As you'll see in the listings below, many sites offer pared-down versions that are similar to the full tests, but the actual licensed versions will cost you some coin. Once you've decided that this sort of data is useful, you'll have to decide if the extra information is worth money to you. To that end, you can learn more about the Meyers-Briggs, and the four-letter personality codes it uses in its results, in the *Wikipedia* article at http://en.wikipedia.org/wiki/Meyers-Briggs. More on the Enneagram is available at www.enneagraminstitute.com/.

HumanMetrics—Jung Typology Test

www.humanmetrics.com/cgi-win/JTypes1.htm

A free test, based on the Myers-Briggs. Answering seventy-two questions yields an MBTI-type report, with their standard four-letter coding. The report comes with a link to the Jung Career Indicator, which suggests careers that a person of this type or that might be drawn to.

When I took the test, the Career Indicator seemed to suggest that I would be happiest as a computer-programming law-enforcing automotive-repairing dentist with a degree in accounting. Links to schools where I could get the necessary training were, of course, included.

CareerTest.Net
www.careertest.net/
Here is another test based on the Meyers-Briggs/Jung typology, yielding the same kind of four-letter code.

The Keirsey Temperament Sorter
www.keirsey.com
Author David Keirsey categorizes people by temperament, using a Meyers-Briggs type of coding ("you are an ENFP"). The types are fully explained on the site.

   You can take the seventy-one-question test at the website, and receive a bare-bones report for free. For more in-depth results, you'll have to get out the credit card and choose one of the fee-based reports, which (as I write) cost from five to twenty dollars.

Career Type Descriptions
www.careertest.net/types/descriptions/index.htm
If you have taken any of the Meyers-Briggs or Jung typology tests and received a four-letter code, then you can go to this page and look up what careers a person with that code might be drawn to. Pretty general, but possibly helpful.

The Enneagram Institute
www.enneagraminstitute.com/Tests_Battery.asp
The Riso-Hudson Enneagram Type Indicator (RHETI) is a personality-style test whose results assign you into one of nine basic personality types. This is the "official" Enneagram site; any other websites with the Enneagram test will be licensing it from this site, so it has some authority (at least to the degree that you feel the Enneagram *has* authority). The URL indicated has a couple of versions of the Enneagram test (and others), ranging from free sample tests to the full Enneagram test, which takes forty minutes and costs ten bucks.

Riso-Hudson Enneagram Type Indicator Sample Test
www.9types.com/rheti/index.php
www.9types.com/newtest/
The first URL leads you to a sample Enneagram test—thirty-eight of the Enneagram's usual one hundred-forty-four questions. It would seem the website creators' faith in the accuracy of this test is no stronger than their grasp of grammar, as illustrated by this quote from the site: "We strongly recommend you to read over the type descriptions after taking the test to see if the type

fits you." Which of course makes you wonder: if you have to check to make sure that the test results fit you, what good are the test results? And how are you supposed to know if the results fit you? Maybe there's a test you can take!

The second URL above leads you to their "new test," which the creators believe will reveal your Enneagram type code in thirty-six questions.

Online Testing: Career Interests

More helpful than a personality test is the career-interest inventory developed by John Holland, called the Self-Directed Search. This test is based on Holland's theory of vocational personality, which states that people can be categorized into six occupational types: Realistic, Investigative, Artistic, Social, Enterprising, and Conventional, often referred to by the acronym RIASEC. The six RIASEC categories (also called Holland codes) are defined this way:

Realistic: People with Realistic interests tend to like work activities that include practical, hands-on problems and solutions. They enjoy dealing with plants, animals, and real-world materials like wood, tools, and machinery. They often enjoy working outdoors. They usually don't like jobs that primarily involve paperwork or working closely with others.

Investigative: People with Investigative interests like working with ideas and thinking more than with physical activity. They tend to enjoy research and like solving problems mentally. They are less inclined toward situations where they must persuade or lead others.

Artistic: Those with Artistic interests, not surprisingly, like to deal with the artistic side of things, being drawn to patterns, forms, and designs. They prefer settings that encourage self-expression, and are comfortable working without a clear set of rules to follow.

TESTS VERSUS INSTRUMENTS

We call things like the MBTI, the Enneagram, and the various skill inventories "tests," but actually, it's more proper to call them instruments. A test is something you can, in theory, fail, while an instrument or an inventory merely returns results without a qualitative judgment attached. Nobody wants to be told that they have failed a personality test; though we have all known people that we suspect have.

Social: People with Social interests like working with and helping others and are drawn toward situations that promote learning and personal development. They prefer communicating to thinking of solutions or working with data, objects, or machines. They enjoy teaching, helping, or otherwise being of service to others.

Enterprising: People with Enterprising interests prefer work activities that involve starting up and carrying out projects, especially business ventures. They have the entrepreneurial spirit and enjoy persuading and leading people, making decisions, and taking risks for profit. They are geared to action more than thought.

Conventional: People with Conventional interests prefer work activities that follow set procedures and routines. They like to work with data and detail, as opposed to ideas and general concepts. They prefer work that has precise standards and clear notions of what constitutes success and failure. They prefer to work where there are clear lines of authority.

The Holland RIASEC code is a three-letter anagram, with the first letter referring to your strongest affinity. For example, if you are most drawn to tasks defined as Realistic, somewhat less drawn to those defined as Investigative, and have some interest in the Social tasks (and are even less drawn to the Artistic, Enterprising, and Conventional tasks), then your Holland code will be RIS.

Just as people can be (at least in a general sense) described by Holland's RIASEC codes, so can jobs and careers. Certain careers tend to attract people with certain characteristics, so it is becoming common for career resources such as O*NET (see URL opposite) to include a Holland code for each job title listed. For example, "electrical engineer" is listed with a Holland code of RIE, indicating that people drawn to this occupation will likely be drawn to Realistic interests first, Investigative interests second, and Enterprising third. Describing jobs this way is not foolproof, of course; if you look around enough, you'll see that different sources assign different Holland codes to the same job titles. So what? It's not rocket science; it's just more evidence to throw in the pile when investigating your skills and interests, and the possible careers they imply. These classifications also help you widen the list of job titles you might want to search for on the job boards, or when using tools like Linkup, Indeed, and SimplyHired.

As I mentioned above, the current licensed Holland instrument (the Self-Directed Search) is not available online without paying a fee. However, there are plenty of websites that have free tests, games, and thought problems that will help you find your RIASEC code. Once you have done that, there are tools that will help you see what job titles your RIASEC code might lead you toward (and possibly, what ones to avoid), along with lists of what skills are involved in certain jobs . . . there's some good stuff coming up.

Holland Codes—Wikipedia
http://en.wikipedia.org/wiki/Holland_Codes
A good overview of the Holland system, with links to typical job titles.

Holland Code Quiz—Rogue Community College
www.roguecc.edu/Counseling/HollandCodes/test.asp
A quick little skill/interest inventory that computes one (or more) Holland codes for you. The results page allows you to see a list of job titles that fit your code, as well as allowing you to see what job titles are associated with the various code categories.

The Career Interest Game
http://career.missouri.edu/students/majors-careers/skills-interests/career-interest-game/
Another RIASEC approach, with links to job titles at the Bureau of Labor Statistics.

O*NET's Computerized Interest Profiler
www.onetcenter.org/CIP.html
This is a computer program that you download to your machine. Once installed, it asks a number of questions, and then kicks back a RIASEC code. It's a bit simplistic, and has an older, DOS-y feel to it—I suspect that it will give some video cards trouble.

Self-Assessment Exercise—North Carolina Career Resource Network
www.soicc.state.nc.us/SOICC/planning/c1a.htm
A more left-brain approach to divining your Holland code.

Target Your Interests—CareerZone
www.nycareerzone.org/cz/assessment/index.jsp
Now that you know your Holland RIASEC code, input it on this page and then click on "View Occupations." You will be shown a list of job titles that are linked to that Holland code. The page will show you similar RIASEC codes and the jobs linked to them as well. Click on any job that interests you,

and get information about it: tasks involved, skills, knowledge, and training required, typical wages and employment outlook, occupations that are similar (*very* helpful) and links to other resources you may find useful. I give this site about a 7 on a scale of 10. It's great at showing you where your interests might lead, but has nothing to contribute when exploring your actual skills or aptitudes. Still, there's lots of information here, and it's one of the best examples of the usefulness of the RIASEC approach.

Career Briefs
www.soicc.state.nc.us/SOICC/info/briefs.htm
A look at many career and job titles, with Holland codes and other data.

The Career Values Test
www.stewartcoopercoon.com/jobsearch/career-values
A quick way of identifying the things you value most in a career, from the mind of well-known job expert Dick Knowdell. Naturally, it's important that your career, and your working environment, match well with your personal values.

Values Assessment
http://career.asu.edu/S/CareerPlan/SelfDiscovery/ValuesAssessment.htm
ASU's list of what is important in a work environment.

Articles about Researching Careers

The following articles should also help you with some ideas on how to turn skills into job descriptions:

High Earning Workers Who Don't Have a Bachelor's Degree
http://stats.bls.gov/opub/ooq/1999/fall/art02.pdf

Top Jobs for the Future
www.careerplanner.com/Career-Articles/Top_Jobs.htm

Top 10 Jobs for People Who Don't Like People
www.freelancer-job.com/top-10-jobs-for-people-who-don't-like-people/

10 Hottest Careers for College Grads
www.collegeboard.com/student/csearch/majors_careers/236.html

Best Paid Careers or 10 Hottest?
www.powerful-sample-resume-formats.com/best-paid-careers.html

Top 10 Hottest Careers List
www.career-tests-guide.com/ten-hottest-careers.html

Career Explorer's 10 Hottest Careers
www.careerexplorer.net/ten-hottest-careers.asp

Highest Paying Jobs and 10 Hottest Careers
www.buzzle.com/articles/highest-paying-jobs-ten-hottest-careers.html

Don't you wonder what they would name these articles if everybody had six fingers on each hand?

Online Testing: Skills

Many of us remember the aptitude tests we were given in school. We should not be surprised to find that there are similar tests floating around the Internet, and that the genre has not improved with age. Some tests have as few as five questions. Wow. No secret safe, huh?

Many skill or aptitude tests are put online by private educational institutions. The results they yield show that you'd be really good at this thing or that, but wouldn't you know, it looks like you're going to need just a few more years of education. Which of course these schools can provide, with your good credit.

Other online tests will have you answer a series of questions, with the results given in a vague, outline fashion. To get the full results—along with a list of careers, any of which will take you to the land of your bliss—you have to come up with some money, in some cases hundreds of dollars. There seems to be a pattern here. . . .

At the heart of current career theory, as introduced almost forty years ago in the first edition of *What Color Is Your Parachute?*, is the notion that skills are transferable from one job to another. Some people have taken this idea and run with it; in some cases maybe a little too far, so that now we have terms such as Key Skills, Motivated Skills, and other inventive ways to differentiate these various skill types . . . assuming there are that many different skill types to differentiate.

When you boil it all down, "Key Skills," "Motivated Skills," and other creative terms are all just another way of saying "skills you like to use." So don't worry about the names or the jargon. The core idea is simple: find the skills you most enjoy using, these skills are transferable from one job to another, use what you know about your skills to define potential careers and job titles when you are job-hunting.

Skills and Abilities
www.soicc.state.nc.us/SOICC/planning/skillsjob.htm
A short overview article about skills and abilities.

Transferable Skills
http://www.soicc.state.nc.us/SOICC/planning/skillsjob.htm
www.professional-resume-example.com/transferable-skills.html
Two short overview articles on the subject.

Transferable Skills Checklist—University of Wisconsin
www.wisconsinjobcenter.org/publications/8961/8961.htm
This is a checklist of various transferable skills, phrased in a way you might want to use in a resume. The checklist has various columns, like where you developed this skill—work? Life? Does it matter?—and whether you want to use that skill in your next job. You can then research jobs and see if the skills you want to use fit that job.

Analyze Your Employability Skills
www.kent.ac.uk/careers/sk/skillsinventory.html
Another skills checklist.

Skill Lists: Creative Job Search
http://labor.idaho.gov/cjs/cjsbook2/skill6d.htm
Another list of skills and skill terms. Ignore the various headings and classifications. Rather, use the list to help get a sense of what your skills are.

Job Skills Checklist
http://owl.english.purdue.edu/owl/resource/626/1/
I'll quote the web page: "The purpose of this skills inventory is to help you to be able to come up with different skills that you may be having a hard time thinking of yourself" after which you would "incorporate these skills into your resume and/or cover letter."

Transferable Skills Survey

www.d.umn.edu/careers/cs_handbook/cshandbook_transferable.html

From the University of Minnesota, a list of certain transferable skills, from the university's *Career Handbook*. The skills listed here are extremely general, and what most people would claim to have. Examples include listening attentively, persuading, solving problems, cooperating, and accepting responsibility. I include this page not because it's a great skill list, but rather as a way to sharpen your ability to convey what your strengths are. As you look through the list, if you feel that you possess any of the skills listed, then do what the instructions on the page suggest: "Give examples of situations when you used each skill and describe specific results." Exactly what a prospective employer would expect you to do.

O*NET's Skills Search

http://online.onetcenter.org/skills/

Most of O*NET's stuff is excellent; this page is maybe a bit less so, though it still has much to offer. From the list, check off the skills you have, and the page will suggest possible occupations. As a skill assessment, it's somewhat general and lacking in depth. The best assessments tend to be a bit artful about how they get to what you are good at; this one, because of its quickness and simplicity, is not. For example, one question asks if you have good judgment. When was the last time you heard someone claim that they had poor judgment?

An alternative way to use this page is to search for, or browse, job titles and look at the skills required, activities involved, and so on, and see how that fits with your picture of yourself. Used this way, it's a neat little tool, and pretty good for finding a starting place.

Federal Jobs by College Major

www.usajobs.gov/ei/jobsbycollegemajor.asp

What Can I Do with My Major?

www.uwrf.edu/career/major-to-career/default.html

Though intended for college graduates, the pages listed here are also useful for finding job titles that pertain to your background, interests, or previous employment, whether you have a degree or not.

Another Approach: The Seven Stories

When it comes to skill assessments, there isn't all that much online; nothing really good, anyway. The skills checklists are helpful, but they are poor at helping you discover what you don't already know about yourself. And that's really what we want any test or assessment, to do: tell us things we don't yet know.

The best way to perform a skill assessment that I know of is decidedly low tech. (Note that this exercise, and other useful ones, is explained more fully in *What Color Is Your Parachute?* and *The Quick Job-Hunting Map,* both by Richard Bolles and published by Ten Speed Press.)

Here's how you do it: sit down, and write a story. The story is about some accomplishment of yours; something you're proud of, something you enjoyed doing. Whether it happened at work or not is unimportant. You are not writing this story for anyone else to ever see, so don't worry about how well you write it, or about spelling or grammar, or anything having to do with style points. Use simple, declarative statements, but be thorough. *I did this. Then I did that. Then I did the next thing.* You just want to make sure that the story includes the following:

- What was your goal? What did you want to accomplish?
- What problems, obstacles, or hurdles did you have to overcome?
- What, specifically, did you do? Include a description, step by step, of what you did to reach your goal, despite the obstacles in your way. Be *extremely* detailed.
- What was the outcome or result?
- What quantifiable statement of the result can you make?

The accomplishment that you write about does not have to be big or earthshaking; all that matters is that you enjoyed doing it. *Parachute* has a good example, about a sort of homemade camper shell my father built when I was a kid and we were so poor we didn't pay income tax. Before I was ten years old, I'd probably seen every National Park in the whole country with the help of that thing.

When you have finished the story, write six more, following the same guidelines. You want to end up with seven stories of accomplishments that you enjoyed. The only person who can judge you at this exercise is you. *You* decide whether you enjoyed doing it, *you* decide if it was a success, *you* decide how to describe what and how it happened, and the quality of the final outcome.

Now: go through the seven stories and analyze them for skills you used. These will generally be verbs (action words) or gerunds (nouns formed from verbs, usually ending in "ing"). As you go through the seven stories, you will start seeing patterns and consistencies in the skills that you used in each case, and the kinds of skills you used. You can use the skill checklists on the web pages listed above to help you pick these out, as well as the following list:

abstracting acquiring acting adapting adjusting administering advertising advising analyzing answering anticipation applying approving arbitrating arranging assembling assessing assigning assisting assuring attaining auditing bargaining blending brazing briefing budgeting building calculating carving charting checking classifying coaching collaborating combining communicating comparing compiling completing composing computing constructing consulting coordinating coping copying counseling counting creating deciding decorating defining delegating demonstrating designing detailing determining developing devising diagnosing directing discovering discussing displaying dissecting distributing drafting dramatizing drawing editing eliminating empathizing empowering encouraging enforcing estimating evaluating examining explaining expressing extracting facilitating filing financing fixing following gathering guiding handling helping hiring hypothesizing identifying illustrating imagining implementing improving improvising influencing informing initiating innovating inspecting inspiring installing instructing integrating interpreting interviewing inventing inventorying investigating judging leading learning lecturing listening maintaining managing manipulating mediating memorizing mentoring modeling monitoring motivating navigating negotiating observing operating ordering organizing originating participating perceiving performing persuading photographing piloting pinpointing planning predicting preparing prescribing presenting printing problem-solving processing producing programming promoting proofreading proposing providing publicizing purchasing reading reasoning receiving recommending reconciling recording recruiting referring rehabilitating reinforcing relating reorganizing repairing reporting researching restoring reviewing revising risking routing sawing scheduling screening selecting selling separating serving setting-up shaping sharing simplifying sketching solving sorting speaking sporting studying summarizing supervising surveying supplying synthesizing talking teaching team-building telling testing training translating traveling treating trouble-shooting tutoring typing understanding unifying uniting verbalizing visualizing welding writing

When you are finished analyzing your stories, you will see what the skills are that you used most; and you'll undoubtedly start seeing patterns, with the same skills appearing in different situations. Since you're analyzing stories about things you enjoyed doing, the skills that keep appearing in your seven stories will be skills that you enjoy using. (Also, see Word Clouds and how to use them, in chapter 4.)

Now, you should prioritize these skills: even among skills you enjoy using, you will enjoy some skills more than others. So put them in order, with the skills you enjoy using most at the top, and the ones you enjoy using perhaps somewhat less toward the bottom. (See Prioritizing, below, for more on how to do this.) Now you have a list of your favorite skills, and they are probably some of your strongest ones as well. When you look at this list, does it suggest any job titles to you? Show your list of favorite skills to friends and relatives, and see if your list sparks any job suggestions from them; the web pages below (and earlier) will also help to suggest job titles and careers.

PRIORITIZING

Prioritizing—getting a list in order of importance—is easy when you have three or four items, but as lists get longer, it gets much harder. The only real fool-proof way to prioritize a list is to compare, one at a time, every item in the list to every other item in the list. It is a process that cries out for a computer.

Luckily, I have one. From this book's website at http://job-huntingonline.webs .com/, you can download a Windows program I wrote that accepts an unordered list, in text file form, allows you to easily prioritize it, and then lets you save the now-prioritized list.

Another approach is to use a web-page-based prioritizing tool. If you go to www.successonyourownterms.com/ prioritizing-grid, there is a ten-item form

available, or a custom n-number form that allows you to input and prioritize any number of items. The only drawback to this web-based-prioritizer is that, unlike the downloadable version, you cannot deal with lists in file form. That is to say, you cannot open a list from your computer and save the prioritized list back to your computer; instead, you must type in your list's entries each time you want to use it, or do a lot of copying and pasting.

If neither of these approaches appeal, or the power company has lost patience with your free-form approach to bill paying, then you can light a candle and use the paper-and-pencil versions of the Prioritizing Grids available in *What Color Is Your Parachute?*, *The Quick Job-hunting Map*, or *The Job-Hunter's Survival Guide*.

You will undoubtedly find a variety of different job titles that fit your skills. Perhaps you can use some of the personality and career tests from earlier in the chapter to help narrow your focus a bit.

CareerOneStop Skills Profiler

www.careerinfonet.org/skills/default.aspx

This web page can be used in a number of ways. You may search by job title, or browse through a list of job titles, that you have had before; the site shows you the skills commonly used in that job, as well as typical activities. You can rate your level of proficiency with these skills and activities. The program then gives you a "skills profile," and an "activities profile," which, though not all that useful in themselves, are helpful in breaking down various job titles into their component skills and activities. Even more useful is the list of other occupations that use the same sort of skills.

The site is also useful for looking at jobs that you might like to have, and seeing if the skills and activities involved would suit you.

CareerOneStop Occupation Profiler

http://tinyurl.com/c6qw44 or
www.careerinfonet.org/Occupations/select_occupation.aspx?next=occ rep&
level=&optstatus=111111111&id=1&nodeid=2&soccode=&stfips=&jobfam

Another excellent page from CareerOneStop, with data on many occupations. Search by keyword, or browse through a list, of many job titles, and see what knowledge, skills, and abilities are required to perform this job, as well as a list of detailed work activities. You can see salary and employment trends by state; education required, as well as the spread of various education levels throughout that occupation (percentage of people in that occupation with two- or four-year degree, percentage with masters, etc), and profiles of similar occupations from a number of sources. Much like the page listed above, but approaching from a different direction.

JOBSTAT—Job Skills Transfer Assessment Test

www.positivelyminnesota.com/apps/lmi/ota/OccupationSelectA.aspx

From the Minnesota Department of Employment and Economic Development, this is not really a test, but a tool. Enter a previous job, and the website returns jobs that use similar skills, with various helpful details. A good way to stimulate your thinking about possible job titles for you to explore.

O*Net—Military Crosswalk Search
http://online.onetcenter.org/crosswalk/MOC/
How does your military training translate into civilian life? Enter the code or title from your Military Occupational Classification (MOC) and receive a detailed analysis of the skills and tasks involved, plus referencing toward civilian occupations.

Military MOS Translator
http://www.military.com/skills-translator/mos-translator
Similar to O*Net's, using the same database.

CareerOneStop—My Skills, My Future
http://myskillsmyfuture.org/
This is kind of a neat little utility. Input a job you have had in the past; the page returns a list of job titles that use similar skills, along with salary ranges, training level, and other helpful information. Also allows you to compare the skills used in your past job with the skills required for the next job, so you can see where you might need extra training.

Tools and Technology Search—O*NET's T2 Database
http://online.onetcenter.org/search/t2/
Another neat web page. Input a tool or technology you are familiar with. Back comes a list of occupations that use that tool or technology, plus similar ones, plus similar sounding ones, plus . . . you get the idea. The database has a wide reach, and is great at helping you think outside of the box.

Vocational Information Center
http://www.khake.com/page5.html
This is an amazing research page, with links to almost *everything*. Job market information, economic outlook, licensing authorities, and so on. Terrific.

Bureau of Labor Statistics
www.bls.gov
What is happening in certain industries? What is the turnover for certain careers? Outlook for hiring over the next few years? Regional data? National data? Costs of employment? Demographics of the labor force? Fatalities on the job? Wages by area and occupation? International labor data? And on and on. *Anything* having to do with work that the government wants to know

is here . . . and trust me, they want to know *everything*. Note also the next two entries.

The Occupational Outlook Handbook
www.bls.gov/oco
This is the bible of occupational fields, put out by the US Department of Labor, Bureau of Labor Statistics, updated every two years, and the place to begin, of course, in researching particular occupational fields. Here you will find descriptions of "what workers do on the job, working conditions, the training and education needed, earnings, and expected job prospects in a wide range of occupations."

The Career Guide to Industries
www.bls.gov/oco/cg/home.htm
Companion to the *Occupational Outlook Handbook;* while the Handbook looks at jobs from an occupational point of view, the Career Guide to Industries "provides information on available careers by industry, including the nature of the industry, working conditions, employment, occupations in the industry, training and advancement, earnings and benefits, employment outlook, and lists of organizations that can provide additional information." I couldn't have said it better myself.

Beyond Skills Alone

When looking online at the various lists of transferable skills, you might easily get the impression that transferable skills are only those skills that one might call "soft" skills. You'll see terms like "active listening," "team building," "problem solving," "information gathering," and so forth.

But practically all skills are transferable skills. Welding, assembling, testing, turning (lathe work)—skills that we might call "hard" skills, or body skills—are as transferable as any of the "softer" skills.

But, while skills are transferable, they are not context-free. You gained your skills under certain conditions and in certain settings. Often, you have used these skills working in certain industries, and all industries have their own customs and practices. When you are looking at career changes, you need to be conscious of the fact that even though the skills used may be the same, the industry practices can be quite different.

For example, a lab tech may move easily from hospital work to a pharmaceutical company, but the practices and special knowledge required in a forensic lab are quite different. An electronics assembler in a manufacturing setting would need extra training before performing the same work in an aerospace company. Practices that yield efficient results in the military are often unsuitable in civilian settings.

Therefore, when examining various job titles and careers, remember that it's more than just the required skills that you need to consider—context counts, too. Every industry has practices and methods that are unique. If you are changing careers, consider how familiar you are with the industries involved. Make sure the careers you target represent realistic, attainable goals. An electrician, experienced in home construction, is an unlikely candidate for wiring the space shuttle.

You may find a number of industries and careers that you can move into with little trouble, while others will be in environments well outside your experience. When moving into a new industry, your lack of familiarity with that industry's practices will define the amount of training you'll need before you can perform your new duties effectively. If your prospective employer believes that you need more training than he can afford, then it doesn't matter how skilled you are. To him, you are not cost-effective. And of course the flip side is true: if your history shows you to be an exceptional asset to an organization, then a new employer might be willing to spend the required time and money getting you up to speed.

In cases like this, where your ability to shift industries may depend on your next employer's willingness to train you, your task is to convince him that you are indeed worth the investment. How well you research the careers, industries, and companies you are targeting will often define how successful you are.

Chapter 4

RESUMES

FOR MOST PEOPLE, the resume is one of the most confusing and discouraging parts of the whole job hunt. No one seems to agree on exactly how to write it, who should write it, what to include in it, how to use it, when to use it, if to use it . . . it's kind of a mess.

And the one thing the average job-hunter knows about the resume is that it's *really important*. He'll spend hours and hours reading books, clicking on websites, listening to advice from friends and relatives, writing and rewriting, trying to get his resume absolutely perfect. And after sending it out over and over again without result, the job-hunter will start to believe that his resume must be flawed. He has to *fix* it. So he'll go through the process all over again. He might even pay someone hundreds or thousands of dollars to write or rewrite his resume for him, only to find that he is still receiving no job offers. It never occurs to him that his continued unemployment could be due to any number of reasons, many of which have nothing to do with his resume at all.

Because the sad truth is that there are times when an applicant is, or is not, hired because she does, or does not, look like the employer's sister-in-law, whom he always, or never, cared for. Or because the applicant looks a little bit like the hiring manager's boss at his last job, who never treated him fairly. Or because the applicant went to USC and the employer has Stanford memorabilia throughout his office. Or a million other reasons, each perfectly illogical and completely human, that, at the end of the day, leave the poor job-hunter still unemployed, just a little more desperate, and with no ideas about what he can do to change his situation. Except . . . maybe if he tweaks his resume . . . just a little bit . . . .

Clearly, the resume issue is not a trivial one. But writing a resume is not the most important thing you will do during your job-hunt, either. In fact, there are many ways to write a resume, and many ways to use it. Traditional resumes, in particular, don't work equally well for everyone, and not all people translate well to paper. For many of us, our work histories appear as our lives have been: complex, fluid, nuanced, contradictory. Lacking the straight lines and purposeful decisions that look best on a traditional resume, we may need to use a different form of this document, in order to reveal our true strengths and abilities, or use a job-hunting approach that places less emphasis on it.

Fortunately, there is no single "correct" way to write or use a resume. Alternative approaches to both writing and using it do exist. If you find that resume writing is not your strong suit, or your imagination needs a boost, there are hundreds of different resume templates available on the Internet that you can download for free. And there are approaches that you can take to the job-hunt itself that will serve to make the resume less critical to your job-hunting success.

HOW OUR MINDS WORK

Next time you're at the grocery store, try this: say you have five kinds of spaghetti sauce in front of you; you will only buy one. As you look at these five jars, checking the ingredients, reading the labels, examining the sauce inside, you may realize that it's *very* unusual to just pick up one jar and walk on. Instead, most people start eliminating: not that one, it has garlic. Not this one; too expensive; this one looks kind of runny. . .

Most of us *eliminate* our choices until we are down to two items, one in each hand; then we choose. If one of the sauces *really* dazzles, then you might pick it at the start . . . but that's rare if you don't have experience with that brand.

The process remains the same whether it's five options or one hundred, spaghetti sauce or resumes. I suspect our minds work this way because primates have had two hands for all the years that our brains were evolving. Notice how human toddlers, when learning numbers, easily grasp one and two, but more is bewildering.

Historically speaking, it took humans a very long time to count past the number 2. This is preserved in a startling number of our languages. Even English reveals this: there is a linguistic correspondence between numbers and their reciprocals—3 and one-third, four and one-fourth, 5 and one-fifth, and so on. But there is no linguistic correspondence between 2 and it's reciprocal of one-half.

To bolster this argument, (and lacking a Latin education) I am prepared to deny the existence of the word "quarter."

But regardless of what kind of resume you use, or what approach you take with it, there are some basic truths about resumes you should know: the resume does not have mystical powers; no one has ever been hired based only on a resume; and all a resume can do—the best that it can *ever* do—is make a prospective employer want to know more about you.

In order to make that happen, though, you'll need to understand that employers and job-hunters use the resume for completely different reasons. To the job-hunter, the resume is a tool used to land a job interview. Yet for the employer, the resume is a tool used to eliminate excessive job applicants. You, for example.

Imagine an employer with a job opening to fill. There he is, struggling under an avalanche of resumes (a thousand applications for a single opening is not uncommon). He needs to hire someone with certain qualifications. It would be great if he could just go through this stack of who-knows-how-many resumes and pick out the few that shine most brightly. But it doesn't work that way.

Most people can't read through a stack of a hundred resumes and remember which applicants had the best training, the most experience, went to the best schools, and so on. Instead, what the employer most desperately wants to do, before anything else, is make this stack of resumes *smaller*. "If I could just get this down to ten resumes—five would be even better—then I could invite those people in for interviews." And so he picks up the first resume, and quickly reads it. (The average resume gets a scan of about eight to ten seconds; rarely more than thirty.) At this point, he's not looking for the best candidate. Instead, he's looking for any little thing that will give him an excuse to throw this resume away, so he can go on to the next one and reduce the pile. **He's not searching for the five best applicants. He's trying to throw out ninety-five resumes.**

If your resume is in that stack, the smallest, most obscure thing could eliminate you from consideration. It's even worse if your resume goes to a personnel department. Think about it: if you were to be hired, it's not these people who would be working with you. No one there even has the power to hire you; that privilege is reserved for the person who will be running the department that has the job opening. So the primary task of the personnel department—the whole reason for their existence, really—is to weed out all but a few of the resumes. The few that survive the process are deemed to represent the best of the applicant pool. These are proudly passed on to the person who actually has the power to hire, who will call them in for interviews. If your resume was one of those weeded out, it doesn't matter how great an employee you would have been. The person doing the hiring has *no idea that you even exist.*

As I mentioned earlier in the book, the Internet has brought a number of changes to the job-hunt. Probably the worst of these, from the job-hunter's point of view, is the increased power of the resume in the job-hunting process. Particularly when using the job boards, the resume becomes the primary point of contact between you and the company you are approaching. The job is a padlock on the company door; the resume is the key. This is very much to the company's advantage, and not at all to yours.

You are left with two possibilities. One is simply to make sure that your resume does not get you eliminated before the interview. This means that the content of your resume has to be *exactly* what the employer wants—no more, no less. Everything that needs to be in your resume—education, skills, experience, whatever—is, in fact, there; and anything that might eliminate you isn't. We'll explore this option throughout this chapter.

The other possibility is to find a different door; an alternate route to the person with the power to hire; a route that does not depend on your resume. This approach has been part of the *What Color Is Your Parachute?* philosophy for forty years, helping millions of people find jobs. We'll be looking at this approach more as the book progresses.

The Job Objective

What you put in your resume is defined by the way you intend to use it. That is to say, resume tactics define resume content. For example, if you are responding to an online job listing, then it's proper to respond with a custom resume that essentially echoes the content of the listing, often called a "targeted resume" or in extreme cases, a "boomerang resume" (so called because what the company throws into the world as a job listing comes flying back at them, essentially unchanged, in the form of resume responses). If you are going to post a resume on any of the job boards, then the content should be a bit more general, because your skills and experience may be suitable for a number of different jobs. You will also need to decide what format your resume will follow: the traditional, historical format, or one of the other formats becoming common, such as the functional resume, the hybrid resume, the competency based resume . . . and on it goes.

Regardless of format chosen, some rules apply to all resumes:

- It should be as short, yet uncluttered, as possible. White space improves readability.
- One page is best, two pages is okay, but never more. That's C.V. territory. (See The Curriculum Vitae, page 62.)
- Never include personal data, other than contact information. No hobbies (unless skill relevant), nothing about politics, religion, marital status, number of kids, or name of dog.
- Avoid phrases that don't really communicate anything, like "passion for sales," or "loves new challenges." Likewise, avoid any general, summary-type statements that are not quantifiable, like "proven executive with unique abilities," or "long history of superior expertise." Rather, quantify your achievements (see below), and if you do that well, the person reading your resume may think to himself, "Wow, this guy sounds like a proven executive with unique abilities." Huge difference.
- Most people need not bother putting the word "resume" on their resume. If you are creating a personal website and want your resume to be indexed by the search engines, then either place the word in the keywords (see page 66), or make the heading "Resume of John Smith." This assumes your name is John Smith.
- Never mention salaries you have received, or salary presently required.
- Don't ever try to explain why you left a job. (See Why You Left, page 64.)
- Do not include your social security number, your home address, or any other data that increases your risk of identity fraud. After you are hired, then of course you would supply such data, but it has no place in a resume, especially if you plan to post your resume online.
- Unless you were home-schooled at the White House, don't bother listing any education before high school.
- Don't ever speak ill of former employers or fellow workers. It was a privilege to work for such terrific companies, and every one of your fellow workers was a rare and wonderful human being.

It's interesting how there are fads and trends even in job-hunting. One trend I've noticed in the last few years is the practice of including a "job objective" in the resume. The argument for doing this is that failing to include a job objective will be seen by the employer as a lack of focus concerning what you want in your life and career. (I do not personally find this argument convincing.)

The argument against the objective's inclusion is less subtle: stating a job objective is saying what *you* want. But what *you* want is usually immaterial to an employer. The employer only cares about what *he* wants, and if your job objective is even a bit different from his hiring objective, your resume will be weeded out.

The place to state what *you* want is in a cover letter, not on your resume. The cover letter is where you can summarize your qualifications and state what sort of position you are looking for. Your resume then backs up your cover letter, showing your qualifications, and proving that you have done and can do the work you seek.

Resume Types

There are two basic ways you can organize your resume. The traditional method is to provide a chronological history of your work experience. This type of resume is best when you have no large employment gaps, you are job-hunting in pretty much the same field that you have been working in, and when the job you are now applying for is a logical step for you to make, considering your work history.

Another type of resume is generally known as the skills-based resume, or functional resume. This allows you to present yourself in terms of your skills, rather than as a person with a certain work history. This type of resume is best when you are changing careers or work fields, when you have employment gaps, or when your past job titles or descriptions do not reflect your true accomplishments and skill levels. Also, if you are just entering or re-entering the work force, you may want to emphasize skills from hobbies or volunteer work; the functional format works better in such a situation.

THE CURRICULUM VITAE, OR CV

Resumes grew out of the more scholarly curriculum vitae, or CV. The CV is a longer document (20 pages is not unusual), more detailed, and one that often allows at least a little whiff of pompous twit to cling to it. It is used as ammunition in academic warfare, to help generate grants, and to impress people who are impressed by people with CVs; for example, people with CVs.

People with CVs don't buy books on job-hunting. Fortunately.

One of the arguments that some experts use against the functional resume is that it may appear as if you are trying to hide something by not including a detailed work history. To counter this argument, some experts recommend what is referred to as a hybrid resume. Your work history is included; it's just not the primary focus of the document.

Regardless of the basic resume form, you can use an approach that Susan Ireland, author of *The Complete Idiot's Guide to the Perfect Resume,* refers to as the Achievement resume. Rather than listing your past jobs in terms of the duties you performed, you list what your achievements were at the positions you held.

Any resume form may benefit from a prominent summary section, wherein you outline your strengths, skills, and experience. Leave out anything that sounds too much like an argument for hiring you; again, that's what the cover letter is for.

As you construct your resume, remember that it must survive the employer's initial perusal, which usually lasts just a bit longer than a winning bull ride. If there is nothing that immediately triggers his desire to toss yours aside, then your resume will get a more careful read. This is where the employer takes more time, checking whether your qualifications and experience fit those established for the position in question. This will be easier to see if you follow a few guidelines:

- When listing your work history, depend less on job titles and more on actions. Don't say what you were responsible for. Say what you *did.* Explain, in clear language, what your job activities were. Each job description should not exceed two or three lines.
- At each job, list your significant accomplishments. Don't be long-winded, but don't be modest. Try to phrase things in a quantifiable form: "Saved the division 2 million dollars over three years," "expanded customer base 12% in first 3 months." State in concise terms where goals were reached and deadlines met.
- Though your education history should usually be listed toward the end of the resume, if you graduated summa from Harvard or were first in your high school class, list these near the beginning of your resume, in the summary section. The same goes for any business awards, special recognition at past companies, involvement in trade associations . . . like that. Remember, the employer is looking for a reason to toss your resume out. You, on the other hand, are looking for ways to pique his interest, and put your resume in the keeper pile. Since you only have

less than a minute to do this, leaving the good stuff for the end of your resume doesn't help.

- Experts don't all agree on this, but you might want to consider a section toward the end of your resume that includes unusual achievements. Examples might be Eagle Scout, having a pilot's license, civic awards, charity work, and so forth. You don't want to brag, and you don't want to include anything that might make the employer think your attention won't be focused on your job. But achievements that say "This is an exceptional person who enjoys challenges and succeeds beyond the norm" can be helpful.

- If you have a long work history, your resume should focus more on the last eight to twelve years. Don't fail to mention your earlier positions, especially if they demonstrate a smooth and logical progression in your career, but concentrate more on recent history than ancient history.

- Remember that employers are examining your resume for ability, experience, and attitude. Your resume should convey these in the most positive manner possible.

WHY YOU LEFT

Don't *ever* try to explain, in writing, why you left a previous company. Not in your resume, not in a cover letter, not in an email. Most people don't write well enough to avoid sounding like whiny, picked-on troublemakers.

Human communication involves so much more than words. Tone of voice, facial expressions, body language . . . we're all experts at divining such subtleties by the time we are three years old. When you give a verbal explanation, all of these delicate nuances are present and cumulative, assisting the listener in empathizing with you. But when putting the same explanation in writing, you give up many of the tools we use to communicate, and thereby risk your ability to connect with the reader.

And of course, you have created and freely given away a document that you now have no control over, with the chance that not all who read it will view you in a positive light.

Finally, whether writing or speaking, don't volunteer your reasons for leaving a position. If asked, try to couch it in terms of a better opportunity coming along for your personal and professional growth, Don't mention disagreements, people who were hard to get along with, abusive bosses, or idiotic company policies.

Listing and Quantifying Achievements

We know that the past is no guarantee of the future, but your history is really the only tool an employer has when he is considering hiring you. To that end, you should try to be very specific about how you have solved the problems of past employers. The person reading your resume wants to know that you can do the same things for his company, and ultimately, make his life and job easier.

With the exception of government and nonprofit entities, all organizations are concerned with two things: problems and profits. To that end, you need to show what you have done for past employers to solve their specific problems or increase their profits. Make a list of what your resume might say to demonstrate your past achievements. Here are some things to think about:

- If you solved a problem, then what was the problem? How was it affecting efficiency or profitability? What was your solution? What obstacles, if any, needed to be overcome? How long did it take to achieve results? Did you do this alone, or as part of a team? Were you a team leader or supervisor? What quantifiable results came from your efforts? Examples might be: "finished the project in half the time previously required," or "my recommendation resulted in a 29 percent reduction in overtime." Try and put a number on it.

- Did you alert the organization to a problem they had not considered solvable, or didn't know they had? How did that streamline production, solve problems, or increase profits? What allowed you to see or solve the problem, when others before you failed? Can you describe what quantifiable results came from your actions?

- Did you increase sales, directly or indirectly? By how much? Can you say you did so "despite the fact that" and then explain an obstacle overcome or problem solved? Did you think of a way to increase the customer base, or reach potential customers never considered before?

- Did you develop any training programs, or increase training efficiency? By how much? Write any procedural manuals?

- Did you invent a process, write code, design an algorithm, or come up with a gadget that formed the basis for a new product, or increased the speed or efficiency of a current one? By how much?

- Did you meet deadlines that were previously being missed? Did you work so quickly and efficiently that you were promoted to a position of greater leadership or responsibility? Can you state that you did something so well that some unusual or beneficial outcome resulted?

Employers particularly love to see instances where problems were solved that were previously unknown or deemed unsolvable, as well as actions or ideas that increased profits and efficiency. The most valuable employee is the one that pays for himself many times over.

If your previous positions were in the nonprofit sector, then obviously profit is not a goal, but other things are: efficiency, being under budget, generating increased donations, securing grants or other funding, increasing efficiency and benefit to the community, and so forth. Much the same applies to government service as well.

Keywords

What computers do quicker than people, if not better, is to say that *this* thing is the same as *that* thing, or that the two are different, and then take some action based on that comparison. This is called the *conditional branch,* and is the essence of all computer programming.

The technology is well suited to seeing if a resume matches a job posting. When an employer is performing a search for someone to fill an open position, he will type in certain search terms. He chooses these words based on what he believes will be in a person's resume. For example, if he needs a web programmer, he might type in "programmer web java html." If any resume in the database contains those terms, then that resume will be brought to his attention ("returned") as part of the search results.

In the early days of online job boards, it was quite an art to write your resume so that it would read well, yet still contain all of the words that someone might use to search with. These are called keywords.

In the years since, we have given up on that particular brand of cleverness. It is now common to place a few of lines of keywords at the end of your resume. As an example, a web designer and programmer might put something like this at the end of his resume:

KEYWORDS computer programmer programming web internet java css ruby html design designer coding bachelor experienced

. . . and any other words he thinks might help an employer find him. Usually, it's limited to two or three lines; four at absolute most. Using more than that looks desperate and unimaginative, but as a result, it's gotten to the point where choosing the keywords has become a bit of an art in itself. When writing your own resume, you can look at the keywords in resumes of people doing the same line of work; or look at appropriate job listings and see what words they tend to use, picking out the ones you think most useful.

Or you can try a word cloud.

abraham action america **american** army article **battle** blockade border britain campaign carolina **civil** confederacy **confederate** congress constitution control cotton court crisis **cry** david davis declaration defeat democrats economic economy ed **emancipation** ended era federal forces **fort** free freedom gen **general** gettysburg government grant **history** http including isbn issue **james** john kentucky lee **lincoln** linge main maj middleton **mcpherson** military mississippi **missouri** national navy **north** **northern** party political potter **pp** president proclamation reconstruction remain republican retrieved rights river scott **secession** seven sherman slave **slavery** soldiers **south** **southern** **states** sumter tennessee territory theater topics troops **union** united victory virginia **war** west william

You've probably seen word clouds before, possibly without knowing that you were looking at something kind of special. They are closely related to tag clouds, and many people use the terms interchangeably, if not correctly. Since the term "tag" has a very specific meaning in computer technology, we'll stick with "word cloud."

Word clouds are an intuitive way of looking at what is essentially statistical data. As an example, I generated the word cloud above by copying a *Wikipedia* article on the Civil War, and then pasted it into a word cloud generator. The generator looks at the incidence of various words, and prints the words that appear often. The more often the word is repeated, the larger it is. In this case, we get this wonderfully intuitive (and quick!) way of seeing the major elements of the war, the reasons behind it, and the people who were major players.

Some cloud generators allow you to assign colors to the words, in order to display various characteristics. For example, most cloud generators accept RSS feeds (an easy way to receive news, blogs, and other data; see chapter 8), and you can assign brighter colors to more recent data.

Not all cloud generators are the same. Using a different generator, here is a word cloud that examines the first few chapters of this book:

As you can see, this one is a bit more "arty," and is not in alphabetical order like the Civil War cloud, but it is no less efficient at conveying information; maybe better. It's really just doing a word count, but manages to very quickly show many of the ideas I've covered up to this point. The words and ideas talked about the most are in larger print, due to their higher word count.

Using Word Clouds

Maybe you're beginning to get an idea of how word clouds can be helpful in resume writing.

It can be difficult knowing what to put into your resume and which words to list in your keyword section. If you want a resume that is statistically likely to match what an employer is looking for, then paste a bunch of job listings into a word cloud generator to see the terms that are used most often. I did exactly that for our web programmer/designer, and here is the result:

It may be difficult to see here, but on my computer screen, I can see a whole list of words and concepts, such as PHP, javascript, Mac/PC, Illustrator, Photoshop, Dreamweaver, InDesign, Actionscript, "strong graphic," "five," and more. (Many of these are languages or development tools.) This cloud gives our web designer an idea of what keywords to use, as well as what proficiencies to highlight in the resume itself. It's easy to get a sense of what is important to employers looking for these skills—they prefer a strong graphics background, and five years seems to be the average minimum experience employers are looking for in this field—and by incorporating information from the word cloud, this resume is more likely to be selected when an employer runs a search for a web designer.

Like all data functions, this technique is subject to the garbage in–garbage out pitfall. The technique is completely dependent on good data, and even more, on lots of data. Small sample sizes are nowhere near as helpful as large ones. The more data the cloud generator can chew on, the more helpful the results will be.

Tag Crowd

http://tagcrowd.com/

A good, basic cloud generator. Allows you to tweak various factors, such as maximum number of words to include in the cloud, and minimum number of times they must appear before being shown. An interesting option is to have the actual number of times the word appears to be listed next to the words in the cloud. I used Tag Crowd for the Civil War word cloud.

WORD CLOUDS AND THE SEVEN STORIES

It might be helpful and interesting to use a word cloud generator with your Seven Stories from chapter 3. Combine all seven stories into a single document. Then copy and paste into a word cloud generator, and set it to work. (Alternatively, most word cloud generators will let you copy and paste multiple documents consecutively before creating the cloud.)

Once the cloud is generated, you'll probably see a pretty good list of your skills. The skills you use most often— you mention them in one story after another—will, of course, appear in larger type. Kind of a quick-and-dirty approach to skill identification.

Wordle

www.wordle.net

Wordle is like Tag Crowd, except that the programmer who wrote the Wordle website sees word clouds as art, beautiful to look at. It's hard to argue with his approach; I used Wordle for the other two word clouds, and not only do they look wonderful, there is actually more information represented in them. As with Tag Crowd, you can tweak a number of factors, but Wordle's tweaks have more to do with changing the way the cloud looks, while Tag Crowd's tweaks have more to do with how the data is processed. Obviously, both approaches have their strengths, and there is no reason why you shouldn't use both if you can benefit thereby.

WordSift

www.wordsift.com

WordSift uses some different approaches than Tag Crowd and Wordle. A nice feature: click on a word in the cloud, and the site will list the phrases, from the data you input, where that word was used. (It is in this case that the word you are clicking on is functioning as an actual "tag," by pointing to associated data. In case you really wanted to know.)

ToCloud

www.tocloud.com

Yet another generator with some neat features.

All of the cloud generating sites I have listed are useful, and they are all different. One thing that most of them will allow you to do is generate a word cloud from a web page or a blog. If you are doing some research and encounter a blog you are unfamiliar with, generating a quick word or tag cloud will allow you to quickly see what is there, and whether it will be useful to you. (In this instance, a tag cloud may be more useful than a word cloud; the tag cloud allows you to click on a word in the cloud you generated, swiftly bringing up the blog entries where it was used.)

These cloud generators are neat tools, and can be fun to play around with, too. But don't get sidetracked. You're looking for a job. If these tools don't help move you toward that goal, move on and try another approach.

Resume Articles

The Internet is a rich repository of resume advice, with many articles and many samples. I have chosen the following websites not because I agree with everything they say (I don't), or because they all agree with each other or share a common theme (they don't). But I *do* think that the sites listed here offer good, sound advice, and represent the upper crust of the resume information available online. Hopefully, my advice in this chapter will help when some of these sites disagree with each other—and trust me, they will—but if you diligently read through all of the material and are still confused about what you should do in a certain instance, just go with what your gut tells you. God speaks in many ways, indigestion not the least of these.

Susan Ireland's Resume Site

http://susanireland.com/resume/how-to-write/
http://susanireland.com/letter/how-to/
Susan has a nice website here, with step-by-step advice on writing resumes and cover letters, with many samples of both. She includes advice on traditional, functional, and hybrid style resumes, and includes examples of all.

Your Resume Guide

www.missouribusiness.net/career/resume.asp
From the excellent Missouri Department of Economic Development, an excerpt from their resume guide with information and advice on a number of different resume formats, including the "targeted resume," a format useful, for example, when replying to an online job-board listing.

Resume Action Verbs and Keywords

www.resume-help.org/resume_action_words.htm
This page has several hundred action verbs and skill words that you might want to include when describing what you did at previous positions.

44 Resume Writing Tips

www.dailywritingtips.com/resume-writing-tips/
Tips on resume writing, but ignore the part where he says you should proofread your resume twice. You should proofread it *many* more times than that.

Resume Writing

http://careerplanning.about.com/od/resumewriting/a/resume_writing.htm

From About.com's section on careers, this is a good basic article on writing your resume. Like many sources, the author of this article sees the resume as part of a larger selling strategy, with you as the product.

Hot Tips on Resume Writing

www.damngood.com./jobseekers/tips.html

From the late Yana Parker's site, The Damn Good Resume. We don't agree on the job objective issue, but the site still has many good points.

How to Write a Masterpiece of a Resume

www.rockportinstitute.com/resume_02.html

A well-written and pretty thorough guide from Rockport Institute.

Resume Templates—Microsoft Office

http://office.microsoft.com/en-us/templates/CT010104337.aspx

Various templates for Word.

109 Free Resume Samples and Templates

www.resume-help.org/free_resume_examples.htm

From Resume-Help.org, a well organized list of free resumes and templates.

Put Volunteer Work on Your Resume

www.utexas.edu/lbj/rgk/serviceleader/volunteers/resume.php

A good article detailing how to do just what it says.

The Resume Guide

www.mass.gov/Elwd/docs/dcs/1865_508.pdf

From the Massachusetts Department of Workforce Development, an Adobe Acrobat document (a PDF file, so save it to your hard drive) on writing your resume, with examples.

Key Resume Enhancers

www.quintcareers.com/resume_enhancers.html

A nice article from the Quintessential Careers site; one of many resume articles at QuintCareers.

Resumes and Vitae Guide

www.career.vt.edu/ResumeGuide/Index.html

From Virginia Tech's Career Services. They've got some nice articles on resume writing. The accent is on resumes for students, of course, but valuable information is to be found here regardless of where you are in life.

Creating Your Resume

http://careeractioncenter.edcc.edu/_jobsearch/resume/Creating_Your_Resume.php

Sometimes the hardest part is getting started. This article is aimed at students, but can be helpful for all, especially if you are having a hard time finding a starting point.

CareerLab—First and Best Cover Letters

www.cover-letters.com/

Turning from resumes to cover letters, here's a collection of them available for free. There are cover letters galore, cold-call letters, thank-you letters, letters helping you to leave a job gracefully, how to negotiate a pay raise, and so on.

Cover Letters—Types and Samples

www.career.vt.edu/JobSearchGuide/CoverLetterSamples.html

From the Career Services office at Virginia Tech comes this excellent article on cover letters, with samples of same, including email versions. Probably the single best cover letter resource I have found online.

Indeed Forums—Resume Tips

www.indeed.com/forum/gen/Resume-Tips/most-people-s-resumes-just-bad/t48415

I include this forum page from Indeed so you can see some of the confusion that resume issues do generate. I was a bit surprised—just about every one of the resume issues I have talked about can be found in this discussion.

The Gateways

Don't forget to check the Gateway and Blog sites listed in chapter 2, all of which are great sources for resume information, tips, and samples.

And Try These Search Terms

resume	*resume tips*
resume templates	*resume examples*
resume formats	*resume writing*
winning resume	*proven resume*

As you can see, there is no shortage of resume advice online. You will also notice that the commercial temperature is higher on the resume websites than it is elsewhere. Many sites will be happy to sell you something—books, help with writing your resume, help with distributing your resume, and on it goes. If you do your homework, you shouldn't need to pay anyone money.

There is a lot of good, free advice available. *Read it.* There are hundreds of examples available for no charge. *Use them.* Often, a website will put up some free stuff, and then manage to give you a subtle case of the guilts for not buying something from them. *Ignore it.* The commerce of the web is such that the website owners *know* that they'll only make one sale for every thousand or more visitors—and they'll *still* make a tidy profit. Let them make it off of someone else.

If you look through the websites I listed, you'll find many ideas on how to write your resume. Soon you'll get a picture in your mind of how you might approach this task. If writing from scratch seems too difficult, then turn to the hundreds of examples; take one and edit it to fit you. They are all there for you to freely use, and there is enough variation that you should have no trouble finding one that will work for you, even if it might require a little constructive rewriting.

Resume Strategies

Make some notes, draw up some outlines, use a template or an example that appeals to you, and then write up your resume using a word processor. Microsoft Word—one of the programs in Microsoft's Office suite—is king of the word-processing hill, and the standard of the industry. If you don't have, and cannot afford, a copy of Word, then you have some options. Probably the best is Writer, Open Office's word processing component. Open Office is a completely free program, compatible in every way with the programs in Microsoft Office. Just download and install Open Office on your computer. (To ensure compatibility with the rest of the world, you may have to change the preferences in Open Office so that Word's .doc format is its default output format.)

Another option is Google Docs; Google has their own software suite, available online. Unlike what you may be used to, the program (what is more properly called the *application*) is not on your computer; instead, the software is online. You can upload documents from your computer for editing or further writing, and it's particularly useful when participating in collaborations or working from multiple computers. (Google sees this approach as the future of computing, where it is unnecessary to purchase software outright. This is also the thinking behind the inexpensive netbook computers you've probably seen. These computers are cheaper to purchase, due to the lack of a hard drive, unnecessary when applications are, and documents can easily be, stored online.)

Microsoft is heading in this same direction with Office Web Apps, but as I write, they are still working on a number of issues, so I can't yet recommend it. But if the other options don't grab you, you should do a search on "Office Web Apps" and see what is available. (Also, by the time you read this, Office Web Apps may be integrated into Facebook.)

Open Office
www.openoffice.org/
Download for free; versions are available for PC, Mac, even Linux.

Google Docs
www.google.com/google-d-s/documents/
You'll need a Google account to use Docs, but you're going to need a special email account for job-hunting anyway (see Online Communication: Email in chapter 5) and Google's free gmail works as well as any.

As you write, bear in mind that this version of your resume is intended to be your best possible effort. It should look good, and be very readable. White space, as I've already pointed out a few times, will help avoid a crowded look. Print it out—reading from paper is different than reading from a computer screen. You should proofread it many, many times. Wait a day or so, and then proofread it some more. After every set of changes you make, print it again, and study it for mistakes or potential improvements.

When you are certain that this is your best effort, print it on minimum 24-pound, high-quality paper, using a laser printer or copier—most inkjet printed documents will smear if exposed to water or coffee drips. When you buy the paper, get envelopes that match in weight and color. This is the version of your resume that you will send by US Post Office, or hand out after your interview.

This is also the version that you could include as an attachment to an email, **if a prospective employer requests it.** Don't *ever* send your resume as an email attachment unless you are specifically asked to do so; and if you are, feel free to question someone's sanity. Sending email attachments, complete with hidden .com files, is a popular and time-tested method that malicious hackers use for spreading computer viruses. Given this, it is very unusual for a savvy employer to request that you send an attachment to an email. But it does occasionally happen. In your response, reference the job you are applying for in the subject line, and in the email itself include a short paragraph or two indicating any previous conversations you have had by phone or email about the position you are applying for.

Even though this version of your resume is not designed for computer searches, you might want to consider using keywords anyway. Some companies that you might mail it to may have adopted a paperless approach to resume filing, which means they'll scan and convert your resume into computer form using an Optical Character Recognition (OCR) program, and add it to their database. Subsequent searches would then function better if keywords are included.

Adobe Acrobat Portable Document Format (*.PDF)

In those rare instances where you are asked to attach your resume to an email, and format is not specified, it is also acceptable to use Adobe Acrobat's Portable Document Format. (On the PC, documents of this type will have a ".pdf" extension.) If your version of Word cannot generate this format, then go to the Free PDF Converter website, where you can convert it to Acrobat, and then download it back to your computer or have it sent to you as an attachment to an email.

Free PDF Converter

www.freepdfconvert.com/

In either case, the converted resume will be sent back to you in compressed (*.ZIP) format, so older versions of Windows will require WinZip or (my favorite) WinRAR to uncompress the file. On the Macintosh, any operating system version 10.3 or later will convert it automatically; previous versions may require Stuffit Expander or similar software.

You can also use this format to allow people to download your resume from your website, and all search engines read and archive PDF files.

The Email Resume

You will receive many requests for your resume to be sent by email (embedded in the text, not as an attachment), so you are going to need a plain text version of it. The easiest way to do this from Word (or a similar program) is to go under the File menu, choose Save As, and in that dialogue box, choose the "Text Only (*.txt)" option. With many versions of Word you are then asked, in essence, "You sure about that?", click "Yes", and your resume will be saved in text only format, without special characters or formatting. A PC will automatically add a ".txt" filename extension; on the Mac, you usually need to (and should) add this extension manually. Either way, be sure it's saved with the ".txt" extension, not least because this will prevent accidentally writing over the original (*.doc) version of your resume.

If this method doesn't work for some reason, here's your Plan B:

- With your resume on screen in your word-processing program, select all characters (the keyboard shortcut is Ctrl-A for PC, Command-A for Mac)
- Copy the highlighted text (Ctrl-C, Cmd-C)
- Open a text-only processing application like Notepad (Windows) or TextEdit (Mac) and paste in the text you copied from the original document (the paste command is Ctrl-V or Cmd-V).
- Under the File menu, choose Save or Save As and save it as a text-only document (choose "Text Only (*.txt)" in the Save/Save As window)

Now, you're not quite done. If you look at your new text resume in Notepad or TextEdit, it looks pretty plain and blocky. If your program allows it, change all of the text to 12-point Times or Courier, sixty-five characters to the line. Now spend some time reformatting it in the text processor, so that it looks something like your original resume. Use asterisks instead of bullets, spaces instead of tabs, line feeds (hitting the Enter key) for white space, and so forth. You want to end up with nothing but plain old ASCII text, yet still readable and presentable. Susan Joyce has written a good article

EVERYTHING OLD IS NEW AGAIN

An unsolicited email resume will go straight to the trash bin. Hiring managers get tons of these, along with all of the other emails they must wade through and deal with daily.

But consider: though it is common for a busy manager to receive hundreds of emails a day, he probably receives very few actual letters. If you do your research well, and identify the person with the power to hire in a company that interests you, mailing your resume to that person might be an effective approach.

on how to do this: (Polishing Your ASCII Text Resume, www.job-hunt.org/resumeASCIIpolishing.shtml).

Once that is done, spend a minute playing around with changing the window size of the program—you never know how big or crowded somebody's computer screen might be. This will help you find any rogue line feeds or other difficult-to-notice formatting problems. When done, save this as "JohnSmithEmailResume.txt", substituting your name for John's.

For most people, the experts generally agree that you should not dress up this version of your resume using HTML, unless you are applying for a web-designer position or something similar. Even then, don't go overboard. You can never guarantee what something will look like on another person's computer, and you want to make sure your resume gets proper consideration.

Now, whenever you are asked to send your resume by email, you can pull up your formatted-for-email resume in Notepad or TextEdit, select all text, copy, and then paste it into your email response at the appropriate place, usually after a paragraph or two of introduction. The subject line of this email should reference the job title you are applying for.

An email resume is used in response to a specific job listing. The listing will tell you how they want you to respond. It is usually by email, but some companies ask you to submit your resume through their website. In such cases, there will be a web page with an appropriate form. Copy and paste your resume into the area specified, just as you would have into the body of an email.

What you must *not* do with your email resume is to start sending it out, uninvited, to every company in the world, a process called *resume blasting*. Companies get hundreds to thousands of these emailed resumes *every day*, and they delete every one of them without a second look. Job-hunters who do this are just spammers, wasting everyone's time, their own not the least.

Posting Your Resume

Now it's time to think about whether you want to post your resume on any of the job boards. The advantage is obvious: with only a few minutes' work, your resume is positioned where it may be seen by an employer or recruiter, and you could have interview requests pouring in with no further effort on your part. And in fact, this does occasionally happen. *Someone* has to win the lottery, right?

But, remember, if you choose to go this route, you need to do so with open eyes. Let me remind you of the drawbacks you should be aware of:

- Once posted, you lose control of what happens with your resume. It can be picked up by pretty much anyone, posted in places you never heard or dreamt of, taking on a life of its own. If you are working right now, it could make its way to the eyes of your boss—people have been fired this way. There have even been instances where, some months after hiring, a person's resume has been reposted without their knowledge, making it appear to the employer that their new hire was still looking to better his lot in life; and then was quickly given the opportunity to do so.
- It is likely that during your job-hunt, you will have occasion to edit your resume in order to target a certain employer or position. With multiple versions of your resume in existence, it is possible that such multiple versions may be seen by a prospective employer. If there is a lack of agreement between the two documents, you might have some explaining to do, assuming you are even given the chance. Additionally, those of us whose skills are, shall we say, widely varied if not finely honed, may be able to write different versions of our resume in such a way that each version, though completely accurate, emphasizes widely divergent abilities. This, to an employer, may seem disingenuous.
- There have been many instances where online resumes were used to further identity theft.

The best way to deal with this is to create yet another version of your resume, intended only for job-board posting. In this version, you will edit your email resume and remove anything that makes it possible to identify you. (Depending on the situation—does your current employer know you are job-hunting?—it's usually best to remove your name as well, or use an abbreviated form like "John S." or "J. Smith.") The only contact information should be the special email account you have set up specifically for job-hunting (again, see chapter 5). Additionally, some experts say that in your employment history, company names should be replaced with company descriptions; so "Bank of America" becomes "A well-known financial institution," and job titles should be as vanilla as possible. Once edited, save this version as "JohnSmithPostingResume.txt." You can upload the file or paste the contents as necessary.

Next, bearing in mind all we have discussed about job boards (and will continue to discuss in chapter 7), you need to decide if and where to post your resume. If you want broad coverage, post it on CareerBuilder and Monster. But consider posting on local and specialized job boards as well. If you are in the tech industry, Dice is king; for government jobs, USAJobs is the official site. Many cities have local job boards, and don't forget craigslist. (See chapter 7 for more specialty job boards.) Do not post *anywhere* that wants to charge you for the privilege. Resume posting should *always* be free.

You probably don't want to post at more than six to eight sites; and you should keep track of where any replies come from. Margaret Dikel of the Riley Guide advises that you renew your resume every couple of weeks (employers often look at only recent listings), and if a certain job board produces no results after forty-five days, remove your resume from there and try another. And finally, remove *all* resumes you have posted once you find a job.

Responding to Job Listings

If you are cruising the job boards, or see a job listing on Linkup or Indeed that interests you, don't just fire off your resume in a Pavlovian reflex. Do some research on the company. Find out if you know of anyone who works there, and talk to them. Which is better, being one of a few hundred resumes that the new guy in Human Resources has to go through, or finding out that you know someone who plays golf with the hiring manager, and setting up a friendly lunch?

If you can't find a personal connection to the company (as discussed in the next chapter), then gather as much information as you can. Look at your resume (you'll be using your email version to respond to most job listings). Is there any minor editing that might make it match the job listing more closely? I'm not talking about being untruthful in any way, but it's possible that you may appear as a stronger applicant if, for example, you were to reorder the skills in your resume so as to more closely match the wording of the job listing. If you are applying to a financial analyst position, leave out the two years you milked cows on the dairy farm. Minor resume tweaking of this sort is fine, but do keep careful records concerning who gets sent what when. After editing, perform a Save As and rename this version of your resume, adding the company name you are applying to in the title. This helps you maintain a record of what was sent, and ensures that you don't accidentally overwrite the original version of your email resume.

After you have done some research on the company, sit down and write yourself a short paper, entitled "Why This Company Should Hire Me." List the reasons you would be a good fit there, and why you want to work there. Convincing yourself first will make it easier to convince them.

Use this document as the basis for your cover letter, explaining how your skills, experience, and past accomplishments make you the ideal candidate for their position. If your qualifications exceed those in the job listing, say so ("You're looking for someone with five years experience; I have ten"). Include email and telephone contact information.

Once you've sent your response to this listing, don't turn off the computer and wait for a reply. Act as if you'll never hear from them again, and continue working all phases of your job-hunt.

Portfolios

For many people—artists, illustrators, models, craftsmen, designers, photographers, web professionals, and more—it is possible to bolster the typical resume with work examples. When going this route, remember that a portfolio is more than pretty pictures: you are proving your abilities by providing concrete examples. You'll find lots of ideas about this approach at the following sites:

Design Ideas—Resume and Portfolio
www.howdesign.com/resume_portfolio/
The most helpful of the portfolio sites, with links to many articles and resources.

OPResume
www.opresume.com/
This site has lots of information about creating a portfolio online, and offers free and paid forms of portfolio hosting, including an option for creating a career website (see next section, Personal Web Pages).

5 Steps to a Better Design Portfolio
http://veen.com/jeff/archives/000935.html
Good advice, with examples.

Portfolio Library
http://amby.com/kimeldorf/portfolio/
Martin Kimeldorf is a well-known and articulate portfolio evangelist, with books on the subject and one of the best websites. Articles, examples, advice, and more. His form is not by any means the only way to go, but it may stimulate your own creativity.

Burn Your Resume, Build a Resume Portfolio

www.eresumes.com/resume-writing4.html

This article argues for trying the portfolio approach, instead of using a resume.

Portfolio and Resume Builder

www.krop.com/creativedatabase/

A portfolio hosting and creation site.

Teacher Tap—Electronic Portfolios

www.eduscapes.com/tap/topic82.htm

The accent is on the digital or multimedia portfolio, but there are many links on many different portfolio aspects. The site is primarily a resource for teachers, but obviously there is lots of stuff here that you can use regardless of your training.

And Try These Search Terms

portfolio advice   *portfolio examples*   *resume portfolio*

Personal Web Pages

Another way of posting your resume is by creating your own website. No family vacation photos, no links to your favorite videos. Just job-hunting stuff: for example, an introductory page, a resume page, and perhaps some work samples. This is suitable for any job-hunter.

Those with an art or design background can use a personal website to publish their portfolio, or to include samples of work. Architects, interior designers, graphic artists, web programmers, application developers . . . any career where such a website can serve as a response to "show me."

There are two basic approaches to hosting a website. You can go the standard route, wherein you register a domain name and then pay for site hosting, or you can use one of the websites that offer free web hosting.

Once the hosting procedure is decided, you can design your own website if you have the necessary skills; many sites offer tools and templates, even Google. Or you can hire someone to do it for you. One of the best places to find talented web-page designers is on craigslist, under the services/computer heading.

When possible, your domain name should be as close to your own name as possible: www.JohnSmith.org, or www.JohnSmith-Jobhunter.com—something along those lines. One problem with using the web space provided by some ISPs, as well as many hosting sites, is that the URL ends up looking something like this:

www.webhostingservice.com/yaddayadda/blahblah/johnsmith/

Which is one of the reasons why I like Webs.com. They offer free web hosting, and your name comes first in the URL, so it will look like this:

www.JohnSmith.webs.com

Much more professional looking, much easier for someone to remember. Although Webs.com offers fee-based packages with greater function and storage, their free package is perfectly reasonable for creating a job-hunter's web page, complete with email address. They have many templates and web-design tools, or you can use off-site page design tools or services, and then load the results into the site. I use Webs.com to host the website for this book.

Here are some sites to learn about and work with personal web pages while job-hunting:

Webs.com
www.webs.com/
The site I've been describing; very well done, and hard to argue with the price.

How Do I Set Up a Website?
www.boutell.com/newfaq/creating/setup.html
To learn the basics of setting up a website, start here. This page assumes you know almost nothing and explains it all well, without trying to sell you something. Other pages on this site are just as good.

How to Create a Website—The Beginner's A to Z Guide
www.thesitewizard.com/gettingstarted/startwebsite.shtml
From The Site Wizard, this is exactly what it says it is. It leads you, step-by-step, through each task involved in setting up your site. Links are included to other good sites, each with a wealth of information.

Creating Your First Website
www.adobe.com/devnet/dreamweaver/articles/first_website_pt1.html
If you have access to Dreamweaver, a popular web-page development program from Adobe, then this site explains in simple terms how you can use it to create the pages for your website.

GoDaddy
www.godaddy.com
Forgive them the tasteless television commercials—imagine the fantasies of a fourteen year-old boy with bad acne, and you won't be too far off—because GoDaddy is one of the best, most popular, and least expensive web-hosting services available. Once you understand the basic processes involved in setting up websites, you can go to GoDaddy's Guides or the Help Center to start making the site a reality. (By the way, the commercials are at http://videos .godaddy.com/godaddy_media.aspx, but since you're job-hunting, you don't have time for Danica Patrick videos.)

Resource Page for Web-Based Resumes
www.quintcareers.com/web.html
An article from the QuintCareers site, with many resources listed.

And Try These Search Terms
create website   *web hosting*   *web page create*

Recruiters

Another way of "posting" your resume is to send it to recruiters. (Grabbing the attention of recruiters is also one of the purposes of creating a web persona, as explained in the next chapter.) When times are bad and hiring is slow, recruiters get hungry just like job-hunters; we've talked about how many of the listings on the job boards are placed there by recruiters as they search the Internet for people they feel they can "sell" to employers. There's no real problem with this, unless you find yourself in competition with a recruiter, where both of you are trying to sell you to the same employer, or a recruiter tries to charge *you* money. Don't enter into an exclusive contract with anyone, and perform your due diligence before letting a recruiter claim to represent you.

Finally, one of the common scams these days involves recruiting firms approaching the job-hunter for a free resume review. "Of course, *your* resume is of very poor quality, but our trained staff will be happy to help you for only. . . ."

If you haven't worked with recruiters before, it helps to know the jargon. An *active* candidate is a job-hunter who is voluntarily working with a certain recruiter or headhunter. (Headhunter used to be a pejorative term for people in this line of work, now it's almost a badge of honor.) A *passive* candidate is where the recruiter goes looking for resumes and candidates that he can sell to client companies (or a prospective client company). At least in the initial stages, the job-hunter is unaware there is a recruiter involved.

Oya's Directory of Recruiters
www.i-recruit.com/
Probably the best of the online recruiter's directories. Listed by specialty, geographic area, and whether the firm typically deals with active or passive clients.

Find a Recruiter
www.findarecruiter.com/
Recruiters pay a fee to be listed in this database.

Net-Temps: Recruiters and Staffing Agencies
www.net-temps.com/staffing-agencies/
From Net-Temps (great site, BTW), listed by location.

The Online Recruiter's Directory
www.onlinerecruitersdirectory.com/
Another online database that recruiters can request to be listed in.

Top 6 Online Recruiter Magnets
www.job-hunt.org/job-search-news/2010/01/03/6-online-employerrecruiter-magnets/
From Susan Joyce at Job-Hunt.org, an article on getting noticed.

EmplawyerNet
www.emplawyernet.com/recruiter/index.cfm
This is a legal recruiters database.

Chapter 5

PEOPLE

YOU'VE HEARD IT BEFORE: we are social animals. People love to talk—*need* to talk, to communicate. When we can't speak face-to-face, we use the telephone. If speech is impractical, we turn to other methods of communication. Facial expressions, sign language, smoke signals, telegraphy, traffic lights and signs, brake lights and turn signals, graffiti, letter writing, newspapers, magazines, billboards, light houses, aircraft position lights, books, notes on the refrigerator, texting, instant messaging, video conferencing, Facetime.

This need to communicate with others is seared into our souls, a part of our DNA. One of the worst punishments we give to our most incorrigible criminals is solitary confinement—simple isolation from other people, communication forbidden. It is enough to cause insanity in a creature that craves the presence of others.

The Internet is just another way for people to talk with each other. Every computer connected to it represents a person. Every website is designed and run by people, with the sole purpose of communicating with other people. Email, chat rooms, forums, social sites, job boards, networking sites. And all of this works to the job-hunter's advantage.

Job-hunting is people hunting. An employer is looking for a person who will do the work he requires. A job-hunter is looking for a person who will hire him. It often takes a number of steps before they find each other, and it is not unusual for other people to serve as intermediate steps in the process. But when you break it all down, job-hunting is a search not only for information but also for people—for human links between you and information, between you and a prospective employer. These days, such links are called contacts, and a common term for all of your contacts is "your network." And, no surprise, the act of systematically using our list of people is called networking.

The experts tell us that job-hunters who use only networking during their job-hunt have an average success rate of between 33% and 60%. That's better than most of the approaches that people take when first confronted with unemployment. And it's an approach that most people turn to pretty soon in their job hunt, too, when a quick look at the newspapers and internet job boards reveals that apparently, Froggie's lost his magic plunker.

That's when they start asking their friends if "oh, by the way, do you maybe know of any openings down where you . . . ? Oh, me? Nah, I was just curious, a guy I know was asking . . ." Then, as time passes, they will turn to their neighbors, relatives, people on the subway, strangers in line at McDonald's . . . desperation is a marvelous motivator. And they might start thinking that this networking stuff is no good at all, but what they are doing is not effective networking.

Effective networking is about establishing and cultivating mutually beneficial relationships. These relationships work best when you are paying it forward rather than begging favors. It's not about you popping up out of the woodwork, taking what you can, and then disappearing until the next time you need help. It's something that you should do constantly. If your present unemployment is prodding you to start developing such relationships now, then keep them up once you have found employment. When things are going well for you again, do everything you can to help and support other people. Not only will it help balance your relationship with the universe, it will also ensure that your calls get returned should you ever find yourself looking for work again.

Like many facets of the job-hunt, networking is not so much an answer by itself as it is part of an overall strategy, geared toward finding rewarding employment. Networking works best when you are using it in concert with other methods to find job leads, to learn of companies that interest you, and to help you find the person with the power to hire.

In many ways, an employer is like a job-hunter. When he has a job opening, he'll want to fill it as quickly, painlessly, and cheaply as possible. Most employers will approach the problem in the following way:

- The first thing he'll do is see if there is someone already in the organization that he can promote into the position.
- Next, he'll ask his employees, and others he knows, if *they* know of anyone that might be a good fit. It won't be someone he knows, but at least this way, the applicant is coming with some degree of recommendation—

no one working at the company is going to suggest their brother-in-law who has a casual approach to personal hygiene and can never seem to hold a job.

- If still no luck, he may turn to the Internet to check the job boards, and use search engines to pick up personal websites and possibly professional associations. He won't get a direct recommendation at this point, but he hasn't had to spend any money, either.
- Next, he may place a job listing on the company website.
- If the previous methods have all failed, he's now thinking that he'll have to spend some money. So he puts a listing on one or more of the job boards, or pays to read some of their resumes.
- Finally, if all else fails, he may take a look at some of the unsolicited resumes that have been sent in. Or not; most companies receive so many unsolicited resumes, particularly through email, that they are often disposed of upon receipt.

The job-hunter wants to find a job as painlessly (and cheaply) as possible, too. So he'll perform many of these same steps. The problem, though, is that the things that are last on the employer's list are the first things that a job-hunter is likely to do, and the first things on the employer's list require more effort from the job-hunter, so he generally does those last, if at all.

What this means is that if the employer is successful in his first few steps, and the job-hunter doesn't progress beyond *his* first few steps, then this employer and this job-hunter will never find each other. If other employers find success early in their first steps as well, then this job-hunter may be unemployed for a very long time.

If you were this job-hunter, what could you do to hook into the employer's approach sooner? Here are a few examples:

- Create an online identity that will make you easier for employers to find. Set up a web page as described in the previous chapter, and use social-networking sites such as Facebook and Twitter (or whatever is popular at the moment) to create a web personality.
- Visit job boards, and job search engines like Linkup, and aggregators like Indeed. Remember, when a job listing looks promising, don't just fire off a resume. Research the company. Do you know anyone there? What can you learn about the company and its problems? Who in the company has the power to hire, and how can you reach that person more directly, bypassing the people who only send in resumes?

- Sign up with LinkedIn. This is *the* premiere business networking website. Everyone should sign up with LinkedIn the same day they get their driver's license. The glue that binds all human relationships is the cumulative weight of common experience. This is true no matter who it is: your spouse, your sister, a friend from college, an email buddy you met on the Internet but have never seen face-to-face, or the co-workers you go out with now and then for a drink. The best networking involves nurturing relationships over time. The longer your history with someone, the greater the ties that bind you together. At LinkedIn, you're likely to meet people with whom you'll interact for many years to come.
- Research companies in your area that are involved in industries that interest you. Find out what their needs are through online research and talking to people in the company. Check sites like Glass Door, LinkedIn, Vault, and Wetfeet. Find out what the problems are that the company is facing, and think of how you might help solve them.

A BIAS TOWARD LANGUAGE

I'm not kidding about communication being in our DNA. Often, where multiple cultures and languages come together (as happened, for example, in the nineteenth-century Pacific when Europeans mixed with native islanders), people develop a simple common vocabulary that allows limited communication; this is referred to as a pidgin. But it lacks form and grammar, and is not a true language. Not until the next generation, when the children—who have a natural instinct for language—get hold of it, will it start developing an actual grammar—now it is a creole. (This process has even occurred with sign languages.) Children's natural instinct for languages starts to disappear soon after adolescence.

Want more? So attuned are we to the subtleties of communication that we perform actions of which we are unaware. For example, you no doubt know that people's faces are rarely bilaterally symmetrical; the left and right sides are often quite different. But scientists have discovered that we emote more with the right side of our faces (independent of handedness), and as a result, people have an instinctive tendency to look slightly left when meeting someone, as a way of gauging mood. This is called left gaze bias. What's fascinating is that when dogs meet people, dogs do the exact same thing. They only do it with people, never with other dogs or animals. Dogs have been around us so long that we have become a part of *their* DNA.

Identify the person with the power to hire, and approach that person as someone who can solve his problems, not a supplicant in need of a favor.

- Look for what opportunities the Hidden Job Market has to offer you. This concept, first outlined in *What Color Is Your Parachute?*, is where you determine what a company's problems are and how you can solve them. If you are able to identify such problems and show how you can solve them, the company will often create a position for you. The best way to do this is by talking to people at the company, as well as those who work for their competitors.

All of the suggestions above involve networking to one degree or another; in fact, it's rare when the job-hunt does *not* involve networking to some degree.

It's at this point that many people freeze up. I know; I'm one of them. As a card-carrying introvert, I rate having a conversation with a total stranger somewhere between having a root canal and being run over by a bus. If you're like me, you may ask your friends about possible jobs, and maybe get a few names from each of them that you might call, but it's not likely that you'll take it much beyond that without considerable psychic pain. Those who describe themselves as "people persons" don't understand how hard this is for people who aren't. But the good news is that networking *does* get easier with practice; and besides, we're motivated. Because in the job-hunt, curiously enough, strangers are much more helpful than friends.

The Strength of Weak Ties

Originally proposed in a paper by Mark Granovetter, the concept goes something like this: most people know between fifty and two-hundred and fifty people. When I say that you know that many, I don't mean that you go out to dinner with that many, or even have everyone's phone number. But that's the number of people whom you can claim as friend, relative, or acquaintance—people you interact with, who would recognize you and your name. Within your circle of two-hundred and fifty, there is your *core*—the few with whom you are especially close, along with maybe another twenty or thirty that you socialize with or see regularly. Outside of your core is the rest of the two-hundred and fifty people you know; these are the ones that you are obviously not as close to, like your wife's brother out in Oregon and that nice older woman in the accounting department.

It makes sense that the people you are closest to will have more in common with you. They will tend to have the same interests as you, and they will tend to know the same people as you—there is a lot of overlap between *your* circle of 250 and *their* circle of 250. And because of that overlap, they will likely know what you know and not know what you don't. And since your "don't knows" are so similar, they are less likely to know of possible job openings, or information that may help lead you in that direction.

It is only when you start getting farther away from your core, and start finding people with less overlap between your two-hundred and fifty and theirs, that you will find the people—and the information—that you and those closest to you are less likely to know. Though it seems paradoxical, it is the people that you know the *least* well who are most likely to be helpful in your job-hunt, by knowing what you do not. This is called "The Strength of Weak Ties."

So when your friends and the people you normally spend time with are unable to point you toward job-hunt success, that is when you need to find the people you do not know well, or at all. The *less* well you know them, the *more* helpful they are likely to be.

Articles about Networking

Job Networking Tips
http://helpguide.org/life/job_networking_how_to_find_job.htm
The best getting-started networking article for job-hunters I have found.

Job Networking Tips
www.enetsc.com/jobsearchtips14.htm
A good getting-started article.

Career Networking Tips
http://hubpages.com/hub/Career-Networking-Tips-Advantages-of-Networking-for-Job-Hunters
A very nice article; his suggestions about volunteering are especially good.

How to Network—12 Tips for Shy People
www.itworld.com/how-to-network-071212

Top Networking Techniques for Job-hunters
www.distinctiveweb.com/news-articles/career-marketing/top-networking-
techniques-for-job-hunters/

Job and Career Networking
www.careerplaybook.com/guide/networking.asp
A short article with some good tips.

Market Yourself Online!
www.infotoday.com/mls/oct01/gordon&nesbeitt.htm
An article by Rachel Singer Gordon and Sarah Nesbeitt. Although written
for librarians, the principles involved are the same for pretty much everybody. The article discusses many of the things we have been talking about,
such as networking, resumes, personal websites, and so forth.

Networking Tools for Your Job Search
www.secretsofthejobhunt.com/profiles/blogs/networking-tools-for-your-job
From a blog by Erin Kennedy, this article lists some of the lesser-known
networking tools available online.

Networking on the Network
http://vlsicad.ucsd.edu/Research/Advice/network.html
Though aimed at PhD students (despite the prevalence of single-syllable
words) this rather lengthy (67,000 words!) article has some good ideas about

THE FATAL FLAW OF NETWORKING SITES

Although there are many networking sites, they all contain a fatal weakness: *not one of them is connected to any other*. The resulting networks are *completely isolated*. In practical terms, this limits what you can accomplish through any single networking site. Likewise, you must choose the networking sites you will use carefully, because you don't have time to actively participate in more than a few, and it's likely to be some years (if ever) before they attempt any sort of efficient integration. For now, all you can do is choose the ones most appropriate to your field, and/or the ones with the most members, and hope that the people you want to interact with have made the same choices.

networking. It is not the prettiest you will find on the web, but there is a lot of helpful stuff here. All of it is good, but if you are in a hurry, skip to http://vlsicad.ucsd.edu/Research/Advice/network.html#section9.

Informational Interviewing Tutorial

www.quintcareers.com/informational_interviewing.html

Readers of *What Color Is Your Parachute?* will be familiar with the critical concept of the informational interview: meeting with someone whose interests are similar to yours and finding out what and whom they know that may assist you in your job-hunt. Quintessential Careers' website has a good series of articles on how to do this properly.

Job-Hunt Networking Articles

From one of the best Gateways, here are two articles about networking: What Network?: www.job-hunt.org/job-search-networking/finding-your-network .shtml; The Point of Networking: www.job-hunt.org/job-search-networking/the-point-of-networking.shtml

ABC News—Dumbest Online Job-Hunt Blunders

http://abcnews.go.com/Business/CareerManagement/story?id=5483048&page=1

I include this for balance only.

And Try These Search Terms

career networking   *career networking tips*
career networking help   *networking job hunt*
networking online   *networking tips*

The Big Three

Networking for the job-hunt falls into these broad, overlapping categories:

Personal Networking: This is the type of one-to-one networking that you do by phone, email, face to face, or with LinkedIn. You are developing relationships between you and other people.

Social Networking: This is the Facebook/Twitter/MySpace approach. You are often communicating to groups of people, rather than the one-on-one approach that constitutes personal networking.

Web Persona: This is about your online personality, developed through your website, blogs, forums, LinkedIn profile, and, to some degree, by way of the social-networking sites. When employers and recruiters go searching for someone like you, your ability to use search engine optimizations, Tweets, and blogging can go a long way toward increasing your visibility.

Personal Networking

The main thing that you need to get about personal networking is that it is not all about you. Rather, personal networking is about your building relationships with people, learning about what their lives are like and what problems they face; what sort of things are happening where they work; and what you might do to help them.

So instead of using people to build up a list of managers for you to spam with your resume, listen to what is going on with people. Ask them for their insights. Gather information. What's bugging their bosses these days? Are their companies coming out with a new product? Is everybody worried about what's happening at a competitor?

Personal networking is not just a white collar thing, either. If you're a heavy equipment mechanic, ask around and find out what company is getting a big contract or starting to build a new section of road; who is leasing some extra graders? They might need more people to maintain the extra equipment. Gather data and make inferences, confirm what you suspect with others.

Finally, I'm compelled to point out that although there are some very powerful networking tools online, in the end, nothing beats sitting down with someone and talking face to face, the way people have been doing since before we were people. There is so much more to communicating than typing and reading words off a computer screen; all of the subtle ways that we interact with each other are missing. The relationships you form online will never be as strong as when you are actually with someone, and even a telephone call beats an email. Bear it in mind.

Forums

There are a number of online places we can go to develop personal contacts. Among the most common are the message boards, commonly called forums. They are often found at websites devoted to a particular subject, field of interest, or function, such as magazines, industry or hobby sites, career sites, colleges, and so forth. At other times the forum will exist as a stand-alone site, in which case, its sole purpose is to allow people to communicate. Most forums will be centered on a general subject or field of interest. If a forum is attached to a host site, then the subject of the forum will be the same as the hosting website.

Take a quick look at these two examples:

- A typical stand-alone forum is MusicBanter at www.musicbanter.com/. The website exists solely for people who want to talk about music.
- For an example of a forum attached to a host website, you can check out Servo Magazine, a popular magazine for hobby robotics. As is typical these days, the magazine has a website (www.servomagazine.com/) where you can read articles, order back issues, subscribe, and so on. Part of the website is the forum (http://forum.servomagazine.com/) where anyone can discuss various aspects of robot design and construction.

All forums have pretty much the same format. The forum is divided into subheadings within the field. You can think of these subheadings as rooms in a gallery, where each room is dedicated to a specific area of the larger subject. So, at Music Banter, there are rooms labeled General Music, Rock & Roll, Rap & Hip-Hop, Classical, Country, and so on. Anyone interested in one of these more specific subheadings can click on the title for access to that "room."

Once a person is in the room, he can read previous conversations—called threads—or start a thread by asking a question or making a statement for discussion. Anyone can read any thread, and those registered with the site (which is almost always free) can post a response to any thread. The response—officially called a reply, what a surprise—can occur almost instantaneously, or it might happen years later, and all replies, chronologically ordered, become a part of that particular thread. The thread itself belongs to, and stays in, the same subheading, or room, where it was started.

Some threads die with few or no replies. Some threads generate multiple replies, replies to replies, and so on, and the thread can go on and on, sometimes for weeks, months, and occasionally years. Threads that the board moderators find particularly valuable can become stickies, where no more replies are accepted, but the thread is prominently displayed near the heading's top to indicate its importance. Often, the stickies are like FAQs—lots of useful information in a small space.

At any time, multiple threads are active, and in theory, *all* threads started since the birth of the board are active, though in practice, almost all threads eventually die from lack of attention. All threads, active or not, are always searchable by subject, keyword, date of posting, name of person who posted, and so on. Which is to say, *everything* that has ever been said on this board, by you or others, is searchable, and *accessible by anyone, forever.* When searching, you should be practical and limit your searches to specific time periods—outdated information is not helpful. When posting, always keep in the back of your mind that what you are typing will be there forever, and what sounds smart and insightful today may drop a few IQ points on its way to next year.

One of the things that you will notice if you spend much time on message boards/forums is that certain people tend to post more often than others, and that the replies to these frequent posters will tend to be extra respectful and deferential. These are the people you should cultivate; they tend to be authorities in their fields of interest. They know a lot about their particular subjects, and they seem to know the other authorities on the board well. If you want to communicate with one of these people only, most message boards will allow you to send messages directly to that particular person; these are called private messages, or PMs. Private messages are not included in the board's database and are neither searchable nor viewable by others. This is how people exchange email addresses and other private information without exposing themselves to spammer harvesting spiders, as well as the general nuisances that sometimes—okay, often— hang around the boards.

All forums have moderators, people who run the board and make sure that everybody stays polite and on point. They can remove threads or replies if they are profane, not in the spirit of that message board, are posted in the wrong place, or if they decide they don't like you. They are generally volunteers, chosen for their superior knowledge of the subject in question. These are good people to know, too.

If you spend time on message boards and get to know the people there, they can be *terrific* places for cultivating contacts. Just remember what Grandma used to say: you never get a second chance to make a first impression, and first impressions *really* count, especially when what you say is searchable and remembered forever. Before you say anything, do a *lot* of listening. Often the people on these forums have been dealing with each other for a long time, and as with any group of people, tribalism exists and newcomers, though welcomed heartily, may be viewed warily.

Probably the worst mistake you can make on a forum is to ask a question without doing a site search to see if the question has been asked before and answered in a previous thread. Such behavior will make it difficult for you to find acceptance and may even open you to ridicule. As with any new relationship, start slow and be nice.

CareerBuilder Community
http://forums.careerbuilder.com/

Monster Career Advice Forums
http://monster.prospero.com/monsterindex

Indeed Forums
http://www.indeed.com/forum

About's Job Search Forum
http://forums.about.com/ab-jobsearch/

Vault Career Discussions
www.vault.com/wps/portal/usa/boards

The five sites listed above are all typical job-hunter forums. You may find other job-hunters here who can provide you with information, particularly about the companies they have left or have themselves researched. Look for people in your same or similar field. Unfortunately, many of the job forums tend to be overrun by complainers, whiners, and clueless people looking for shortcuts. Obviously, such people are not helpful contacts. But as with so much in life, exceptions abound.

On balance, I think you are probably more likely to make useful contacts at forums that are specifically related to the industry or field of interest that you are targeting for your job-hunt; these forums will normally be found on the websites of industry magazines, associations, or even large companies in that field. If the search engines and directories listed below cannot help, then try using your favorite search engines and searching on something like "[name of industry] forum," "[subject] message board," or "[field of interest] discussion group." Use your imagination. Also, try searching lists of periodicals and industry magazines and newsletters, and then checking their websites.

Boardtracker
http://www.boardtracker.com/
This is a pretty nifty search engine. Enter a subject, and it will search through its database of forums to see if there is a thread that matches your subject. You can also go to the forum that was the source of the thread and look for more stuff that might interest you, and make contacts thereby.

BoardReader
http://boardreader.com/
Boardreader is another search engine designed to find forums and message boards. It is not flawless, but it is often helpful.

Big Boards
http://directory.big-boards.com/
This is a directory of forums and message boards organized by subject. They lean toward the large and popular forums. That may not be the best thing for you, but of the forum directories available on the web, this is (as I write, at least) the most complete.

Yahoo! Groups—Business and Finance
http://finance.dir.groups.yahoo.com/dir/Business_Finance/
By *group* what Yahoo! means is very similar to what we would call a forum, except that there is not usually a moderator to keep things under control. Yahoo! has thousands of these groups: industries, hobbies, personals, careers. Tons. If you look where I have directed, under Business and Finance, many of the groups you will find were created for networking in specific industries.

craigslist
www.craigslist.org
Every city has their own craigslist, and every craigslist has a forum area set aside for discussion; you'll see it under "discussion forums." "Jobs" is one of the seventy-two topics currently listed, but not necessarily the best one for your purposes. If the forums don't bear fruit, consider putting a post in the appropriate "community" area.

And Try These Search Terms
career forum　　　　　　　　*career message board*
industry forum　　　　　　　*forum directory*
message board　　　　　　　*directory message board*

Wikis

Wikis are collaborative websites, where any number of people can contribute. The most well-known, of course, is *Wikipedia*, the collaborative encyclopedia. Wikis are a great place to find people with common interests, as well as a certain amount of authority (or at least, one would hope, competence) in their field.

If you are feeling a little skeptical about wikis as a place for finding contacts, take a minute and go to is *Wikipedia*'s "Community Portal" page and just look at all of the projects, collaborations, and teams there are. This is a gold mine of contacts, united by common interests.

Wikipedia is not the only wiki on the web; it's just the biggest. For example, check out Wikiversity, one of Wikipedia's companion sites. Although the site may be less developed than Wikipedia, that's not necessarily a bad thing for your purposes.

To find other wikis, you can use Wiki—the wiki search engine listed below—or use a general search engine, combining a field of interest with the term "wiki" and see what pops up.

Wikipedia's Community Portal page
http://en.wikipedia.org/wiki/Wikipedia:Community_portal

Wikiversity
http://en.wikiversity.org/wiki/Wikiversity:Browse

Wiki
www.wiki.com/
A search engine for wikis. Who would have thunk it?

Personal Networking and Connection Sites

The web has many, many sites that are specifically set up for networking and connecting people with each other. Examples are LinkedIn, Facebook, Ryze, MySpace, and Classmates.com. Each is a bit different from the others, but all have been set up in acknowledgment of the power of personal connections in business, as well as many other aspects of life; job-hunting not the least of these.

Although the concept is powerful, it is not perfect. As I have said, the strongest relationships are the ones that consist of common experience *over time*. Studies have shown that the people who use these sites tend to fall into two groups. The first group includes people who join these sites and participate quite a bit at first, but then their site visits become more infrequent. As a result, the relationships they form there lack depth, stability, and longevity. The other group of users (and the smaller of the two) consists of the people who do keep at it, and as a result, form more lasting bonds with a greater number of people.

If you think you are likely to be a member of the first group, then these sites might not be your most effective approach to networking. We are drawn to those who share our interests; with whom we have something in common. If you are just going to the networking sites to quickly find a job, then all you really have in common with the people there is a certain amount of ambition and a desire to better your employment position. If you approach someone under those conditions, then it will feel (to both of you) like you are begging a favor. In which case, you need to stand in that person's shoes for a minute, and think: would you rather do a favor for a friend of a friend of a friend—someone you don't really know, and don't have much in common with—or someone who shares your love of woodworking, or gardening, or teaching elementary school, or what have you?

It seems to me that unless you are prepared to integrate continued, purposeful networking into your life, you may find greater success if you think of other ways to hook up with people who share your interests. These could be work-based interests—if you are a video-game programmer, then find a forum or chat room where video-game people hang out—or they could be hobby-based interests. You could still be a video-game programmer, but if you really like music, or woodworking, or flying radio-controlled airplanes on the weekends, go to forums dedicated to those subjects, and make contacts there. You will be much more likely to find lasting relationships when there is something you genuinely have in common with people, especially when it touches your enthusiasms. These are the people who will really want to help you, far more than the stepfather of your ex-brother-in-law's next door neighbor.

Of course, if you belong to the other (smaller) group, and are the type of person who is likely to take to and stick with this networking thing, then you will not only enrich your life with the relationships you gain but you'll also be in a much better position next time you find yourself unemployed. (On average, people, change jobs every three to five years.) If you already have a network in place, you will have built relationships, enjoyed common experiences, and will yourself have given help to others, "paying it forward." It will make finding your next place of employment that much easier.

The bond of common experience is also the driving force behind websites like Classmates and corporate or military alumni sites. These sites can yield good contacts for you because, in a sense, these are people you already "know," and with whom you have common experiences. College alumni, in particular, feel a sense of duty toward their school's other graduates, and are valuable resources.

LinkedIn
www.linkedin.com/

LinkedIn is nothing less than *the* premiere business networking site. It is also the most popular: eighty-five million members as I write. And for good reason: it is superior in almost every way to anything else you will find of this nature. It is well designed and well run; the people running it are experienced, knowledgeable, and smart.

When you sign up (registration is free), you enter your basic information—field, job title, geographic area, and so on—and indicate what kind of connections you are looking for and what kind of incoming contacts you are willing to accept. For example, if you currently own a business, you could indicate that you are open to inquiries about employment at your business, but naturally you don't want people sending you job offers for yourself.

You then go on to invite people to enter your network—you cannot draw people in unless they actively want to be included. As the people that you know join, and the people *they* know join, your network grows. At LinkedIn, your network is defined as a maximum of four levels, or degrees, out to a friend of a friend of a friend of a friend. For example, if only five people join at each level, that is still a network of 625 people. In reality, it is likely to be far more.

LinkedIn also allows you to contact people who are not in your network, if they have said they are willing to accept such contacts, and naturally, you may allow such contacts, as well. As is increasingly common, the site also offers "premium" memberships at various levels that include other services.

This is a business networking site, not a job-hunting site. But job-hunting and career change are a huge part of business, and many of LinkedIn's registrants consider themselves job-hunters, even if their current employers do not. LinkedIn offers many features for job-hunters. Some job boards, like the SimplyHired job aggregator, hook in to the site so that when a company name comes up in SimplyHired, you can quickly see if anyone in your

LinkedIn network works there. At the moment, LinkedIn also has its own job board on site.

LinkedIn is also a valuable facet of your web persona, sometimes called your social brand. Often, before calling someone in for an interview, an employer will do a web search on the person in question, and that often starts with their LinkedIn profile. There's more about LinkedIn down below.

Ryze
www.ryze.com
Ryze is like LinkedIn in some ways, very different in others. As with Linked-In, you set up a profile page, and invite others to join. On their "networks" page (www.ryze.com/networks.php), you'll find over 1,000 groups you can join; these are forums, dedicated to various subjects, or centered on host organizations. Acceptance is instantaneous and meeting people there is very easy. As I write, Ryze claims 300,000 members. Not as many as LinkedIn, certainly, but still not too shabby.

Brazen Careerist
www.brazencareerist.com/
This is a fairly young networking site, from writer Penelope Trunk, named after her blog and book. It's kind of a cross between LinkedIn and Ryze. Intended for the younger crowd, it will be interesting to see how the site develops over time. (And how could you not root for a site with such a cool name?)

Weddle's Professional Associations
www.weddles.com/associations/business.htm
Where are you likely to find those who are doing what you want to do? This is a terrific list of professional associations, from the site of one of the masters of the job-hunt and the web.

Corporate and Company Alumni Groups
www.job-hunt.org/corporate-alumni-networking/company-alumni-networking-groups.shtml
This is a list of websites and addresses at Job-Hunt, rather than a single site. People who have worked at various companies—common experience, right?—have set up different ways to keep in touch and get in touch with others who have worked there; or who want to talk about it, possibly network for future employment . . . motives and results vary. Some of the places listed will be

websites, some may be LinkedIn or Yahoo! Groups; it's an eclectic collection, and possibly of value to you.

Veterans and Military Alumni

www.job hunt.org/veterans job search/military-alumni-groups.shtml
Another page from Job-Hunt, listing various military-oriented alumni websites.

Military.com Buddy Finder

www.military.com/buddy-finder/
Enter name, service, and pay grade of someone you served with, and this site claims it can find him or her.

Classmates.com

www.classmates.com/
Well, their marketing campaign is kind of pushy, but there are a huge number of people registered at this site. After all, most of us did go to school, to one degree or another.

US Colleges and Universities

www.utexas.edu/world/univ/
The alumnae organizations from the various colleges and universities are also terrific places to find contacts. This page lists links to colleges and universities in the United States, including community colleges. Go to the individual websites to find the alumnae groups.

Yahoo! Groups

http://groups.yahoo.com/
It's unfortunate that Yahoo! Groups has developed a reputation as a bit of a dinosaur. Because people do still go here; just not to the degree that they used to. The best thing for you to do is browse through and find the groups that interest you—there are thousands to choose from—and see how current they are. If a group interests you, but the last post was three months (or years) ago, move on.

Schoolnews.com

www.schoolnews.com/
The goal of the site is to be a directory of the graduates from over 30,000 high schools in the United States and Canada. Graduates must sign in to

their database; they are not automatically added from registration rolls. Not as good a resource as Classmates.com.

Company of Friends
www.fastcompany.com/page/company-friends-faq
Fast Company is a magazine that focuses on innovative companies and technologies; Company of Friends is a site they set up to, in part at least, help readers of the magazine connect with each other.

The Bush-Cheney Alumni Association
www.43alumni.com/
If you worked for the Bush White House, were appointed to a post under that administration, or were involved in either of the campaigns, you are welcome to join the Bush-Cheney Alumni Association, and network with those of similar background who are not currently incarcerated.

More LinkedIn

LinkedIn knows that out of the eighty-five million (or so) people registered, many will be job-hunters, and so the site has many goodies to help with yours.

LinkedIn Answers is where you can submit a question to your network, or answer questions and help cement yourself as an authority (see Web Persona, page 110).

Company Profiles is a database of companies and information about them. Some of the information is basic in nature—sales, NASDAQ, employees, recent news articles—while some stuff is a goldmine. Recent hires, with the companies they came from, their new job titles, their LinkedIn profiles . . . yowza. See the possibilities?

You can search for a company by name or browse through their list of over 100,000 companies. You may "follow" those companies that interest you, and be notified when job openings occur or when an employee is hired, promoted, or leaves.

Another goodie is the LinkedIn toolbar, which you can download from the site (scroll *waaaay* down to the bottom of any page and click on "Tools"). The toolbar becomes part of your browser allowing you more direct connection with the LinkedIn site and access to some features not otherwise available.

For example, JobsInsider, a feature that allows you to go to certain job boards (examples include sites such as Indeed, SimplyHired, Dice, and the

Supersites) and click on a job listing, which causes anyone in your network who works there to appear in a side panel on your screen. (SimplyHired itself has a similar feature.)

Finally, while basic LinkedIn membership is free, they do offer certain premium memberships, with more services and access to information not available in their standard free package. One of these premium membership levels is specifically aimed at job-hunters; you'll have to weigh the benefits and see if it is worth it in your situation. My feeling is generally against pulling out the credit card. With so much on the Internet (and LinkedIn itself) freely available to the job-hunter, you should see some strong, definite, and immediate advantage to spending money, even at such a high-quality site.

And Try These Search Terms

linkedin	*linkedin strategies*
linkedin job hunt	*linkedin groups*
linkedin networking	

Social Networking

Social Networking, particularly as represented by LinkedIn, Facebook, and Twitter, is the fastest growing facet of the Internet at the moment. Facebook is the #2 website in the world, right behind Google. Twitter is also extremely popular. And though it was not their creator's original intention, both sites are being leveraged for job-hunting.

There are three ways that these sites can be helpful in the job-hunt:

- As part of your web persona
- As a way of networking with others
- To obtain job listings. Jobs are being announced in tweets, and companies are putting company pages, and occasionally job openings, on Facebook.

Because of social networking's rapid growth, the relative youth of these sites, and the lack of history in using these sites for job-hunting, it's hard for me to tell you exactly how to use these sites in a way that I know will be relevant by the time you read this. So I'm going to list some sites that I believe are helpful and likely to stay that way for a while, but beyond that, you're better off doing some quick searches to find the timely and relevant advice you'll need when it comes to this aspect of your job-hunt.

Twitter

http://twitter.com/

The famous mini-blog site, with 175 million (or more) registered users. All entries, called "tweets," must be 140 characters or less. On Twitter, you can post your own tweets, or "follow" other people; that is, read their tweets. Originally, the purpose of the site was just so people could tell their friends what they were doing at the moment. Then people started using it in more inventive ways; the first clever use that I remember hearing about was a woman who had a business where she sold cookies out of her van, like a lunch truck. She would move the van around during the day, tweeting where she was going to be. Her customers would follow her online to find her location and would then, um, follow her.

Over time, equally clever people wrote small computer programs that would analyze people's tweets, collecting the data about where they were and what they were doing, and then used this information to burglarize their houses, knowing no one was home.

Now, clever employers realize that instead of paying $300 to post a job on a job board, they can tweet it . . . or at least 140 characters of it.

As this book was going to press, Twitter was undergoing a major revamping of the site, allowing greater connectivity to other sites and more types of media on site.

Facebook

www.facebook.com/

Originally a college site, based on the simple question: What's on your mind? The site is a terrific way for people to talk to a lot of people at once, so it's great for publicizing events, advertising for a business, and maybe notifying others of a job opening.

Networks are created by people "friending" one another. Like MySpace, everyone gets a Home Page, and many types of media can be uploaded to your page—video, pictures, web links, and so forth. As I write, most analysts feel that the site has reached saturation in the US; 70% of all Americans with Internet access are registered on Facebook, and in December of 2010, Americans spent an aggregate 94,000 years on the site.

At the moment, Facebook has a very casual feel to it. LinkedIn is where people go to do business, Facebook is where people go to have fun and talk to friends. But that may be changing. Facebook has added a Marketplace feature, where you can buy and sell merchandise, and many companies are creating Facebook pages, wanting to extend their reach to more people. There is even a Jobs section (see below). But Facebook has yet to figure out exactly how to efficiently (and completely) monetize its astounding popularity, and so its future form, as I write, is anyone's guess.

MySpace
www.myspace.com
Once iconic, not yet irrelevant; it's hard to say how MySpace will respond to the huge challenge Facebook has presented them with. As I write, the site is trying hard to be a major player again, and who knows what the future might bring? By the time you read this, it might be on top again, or you may encounter a "Page Not Found" error.

TwitJobSearch
www.twitjobsearch.com/
This is a search engine that looks through tweets to pull out job listings. A well-designed and well-managed site.

TweetaJob
http://tweetajob.com/
Sign up at the site to receive relevant job listings culled from tweets.

TweetMyJobs
http://tweetmyjobs.com/
Essentially a job board that encourages employers to post job listings with them at far lower prices than other job boards; the jobs are then disseminated through social media.

Facebook Marketplace/Jobs
http://apps.facebook.com/marketplace/searchapp/?c=job&country=USA
www.oodle.com/
Facebook has an area called the Marketplace, where you can sell and buy stuff, and where jobs are posted as well. It is run in partnership with Oodle .com; some of the jobs are placed by people with Facebook pages, but most of the ones I saw came from a job aggregator, pulling posts off of Indeed and other job sites.

delicious

www.delicious.com/

This is a kind of anonymous networking, not talking to people per se, more like looking over their shoulder to see what they are doing—the site calls it social bookmarking. People share their favorite websites, dealing with myriad subjects. Sometimes, the subject is directly useful to your job-hunt; sometimes less directly so, and sometimes no help at all. A quick search of the site will reveal if anything useful has been posted lately.

Articles about Social Networking Sites

In order to get up to speed on using social networking in your job-hunt, try the following articles:

Facebook Becomes a Job Search Engine

http://recareered.blogspot.com/2010/06/facebook-becomes-job-search-engine
.html

The article title may actually be a bit of a play on words; the article itself is about integrating the SimplyHired job aggregator with Facebook. Well written and thoroughly explained.

Can Social Networking Bring Job-hunters Success?

http://www.guardian.co.uk/money/2010/feb/20/social-networking-twitter-
job-hunting

Good article on social media and networking

9 Job-hunting Tips for Facebook Users

www.moolanomy.com/2346/9-important-job-hunting-tips-for-facebook-users-
cford10/

About.com—Social Networking

http://jobsearch.about.com/od/onlinecareernetworking/Career_Social_
Networking.htm

An article with links to a lot more, each concerned with an aspect of social networking, including job-hunting. About's articles often lack depth, but there sure are a lot of them.

MY PRIVACY RANT

Few of us read the User Agreements or Terms of Use which many websites require us to acknowledge in their signup process. But you can safely bet that these agreements give the user few rights, while the website retains for itself complete absolution for anything less than the act of an angry god.

For years, many websites that we visit have been taking information from our web browsers about what other Internet sites we visit (found in our browser's history and cookies). This information is then sold to others, who use it to determine trends and create targeted advertising (about 80% of all web ads are targeted, using this data). Information about our habits, interests, and concerns is like gold to advertisers, saving money and increasing profits. Unless we take the time to read the Terms of Service for every website we visit, there is no way for us to know when such data is being collected (or, more plainly said, taken) from us. And so far, the only solutions proposed involve asking these websites to not track our movements, and then trusting them to comply.

Of course, besides the websites you visit, targeted advertising would be even more accurate if companies could know about your likes and dislikes, the things you enjoy doing, what interests you have, who your friends are (and their likes and dislikes), and what websites you enjoy and recommend. Kind of sounds like Facebook, doesn't it?

Facebook has been roundly criticized on a number of occasions in the last few years for its lack of sensitivity to privacy issues and arrogance about who owns the data posted on the site. Mark Zuckerberg, Facebook's founder, has stated that privacy is "no longer a social norm", and believes that Facebook should respond accordingly. Since Facebook is working to integrate itself with other Internet activities, including email, its attitude toward privacy issues is no small matter.

Breaching people's absolute right to privacy (which is not stated in the Constitution, only implied) is a very slippery slope. More and more, you are defined by what is on computers around the world. Since current law is far behind the technology, it is left up to you to do whatever you can to protect your Internet data and subsequent identity; laws are unlikely to change until lives have been ruined. It may look benign and civilized, but in many ways, the Internet is like the wild, wild West.

And Try These Search Terms

In these searches, use your imagination. Replace "facebook" with "twitter" and any other site names that may be popular at the moment. Look through the social networking sites and see what has been added to help the job-hunter.

facebook careers
facebook job search
social networking
social networking job search

facebook job hunt
facebook jobboard
social networking job hunt

Web Persona

Your web persona is the personality you project online. It is similar to, and overlaps with similar concepts, such as personal brand and social brand. Put simply, your web persona is the person that people perceive you as, through your presence online. This can be through a personal website, from your interactions on social networking sites, blogs you have written, things said about you online, pictures of you, videos . . . everything. Your ability to control this online image is crucial, and you should exercise this control in two directions: first, by actively creating a very positive online presence, so that you will impress employers and attract those who can assist you in your job hunt; and of course you also will want to block or remove any negatives that will scare people away.

Recruiters often go looking for people when they have a contract to fill, or know of openings that will earn them a fee if they find a suitable candidate. There's no reason why you shouldn't use your online personality to attract recruiters, who are hungry to sell appropriate candidates to employers.

And certainly employers are not idiots; they know how to use Google and do their due diligence on people they are considering hiring. Therefore, you want your web persona to appear serious, responsible, and employable. If your friends start posting Facebook pictures from college, and tagging you in that picture where you were running around with only a pair of underwear (on your head), it may affect your future career direction. Enlist their help in keeping it clean, or de-friend them.

Consider creating a personal website, as described in chapter 4. Use it to point toward your LinkedIn profile and Facebook page. (Your LinkedIn profile and Facebook page can also point to your personal website.) With all of these sites interconnected, make sure that all data is current, positive, and consistent.

Once your website is to your satisfaction, set up your LinkedIn profile. Google indexes these, so when an employer is looking for someone, or is researching you to consider bringing you in for an interview, this could be one of the first things that pops up. This could well be your chance to make that first online impression. Consider adding your LinkedIn profile to your Facebook page (instructions are at www.facebook.com/apps/application .php?id=6394109615&v=info) and read the following articles:

LinkedIn Learning Center—Profiles
http://learn.linkedin.com/profiles/

LinkedIn Profile Extreme Makeover
http://blog.guykawasaki.com/2007/01/linkedin_profil.html#axzz16FyVqM2z

5 Steps to a Fantastic LinkedIn Profile
www.lindseypollak.com/archives/how-to-have-a-fantastic-linkedin-profile

Use Your LinkedIn Profile as a Resume
http://jobsearch.about.com/od/networking/a/linkedinprofile.htm

Increasing Your Visibility

Once upon a time, before most people had computers in their homes, I was a luthier, which is a person who makes stringed musical instruments. I wasn't the best; I wasn't the worst. Like other luthiers, I advertised a little, depended on a lot of word of mouth, and eked out a living.

Then I started writing for industry publications, creating articles helpful to both musicians and other luthiers. In a surprisingly short time, I became extremely well known in my field. I've now been out of the business for over twenty years, but in great part because of the articles I wrote and the industry visibility I created, I'm as well known now as I was then. Maybe better.

Today, the Internet makes it much easier to do what I once did. There are three approaches you can take:

1) Be a forum presence. Find the forums appropriate to your industry, become familiar with the issues on site, and slowly start showing your voice. The same applies to LinkedIn's Groups, Facebook Groups, and any other places of visibility where your knowledge and experience can help to make your voice one of authority.

2) Write a blog. You can post it on your personal website, or use one of the blog hosting sites. Obviously, you're not just doing this to hear your own voice; be helpful. Address problems that face people in your field. Do some reading on search engine optimizing, and use that to increase the visibility of your blog during searches.

3) Comment on other people's blogs. Find the authorities in your field, and comment on the blogs that they write. This is actually the first thing you should do out of the three; it is the quickest way for you to become familiar with some of the authorities in your field, and they with you.

Blogging is not a one way street; it is, at least in part, a dialogue. People don't just write blogs and forget about them. They read the comments that others make to get new ideas, and to show themselves that other people are reading what they have taken the time and effort to write. Eventually, you'll get a sense of what you should write about, and as you conduct a dialogue with the authorities in your field, one day you may wake up to find you are one of them. Not only is this networking on a high level, it also builds your web persona, increasing your visibility.

Obviously, you shouldn't stop blogging when you find employment. Your increased visibility and authority will make you that much more valuable to your present employer, and more desirable to future ones.

Blogger
www.blogger.com
www.blogger.com/features
Probably the best of the blog hosting sites; check the second URL to see some of the features offered at the site, including the possibility of maybe making some money at it.

WikiHow—How to Start a Blog
www.wikihow.com/Start-a-Blog
A good article on getting started.

And Try These Search Terms
blog hosting *how to blog*
start blog *blog visability*

Video Visibility

Another way of defining your web persona is by putting videos on YouTube. If what you do well translates to video, then get a knowledgeable friend (or hire a pro) and make some videos that help you look like an authority in your field, and put them on YouTube. YouTube videos can also be linked to your personal website and Facebook page. When you do this, **make sure that your name is part of the video title.**

As my kids might have once said, don't look like a doofus. You don't want to post videos if you are just going to stand at a lectern and talk about international exchange rates. But if you can translate your skills into a visual presentation—think video portfolio, or video blog, with visual interest—then this will add to your online persona. There are articles all over the web on how to do this sort of thing; search for them and see if this appeals to you.

Looking for People Online

Here are a number of tools for finding somebody when you have a basic idea of who it is you are looking for. Some of these sites, like ZoomInfo, Intelius, US Search, and ZabaSearch, use many of the same tools and techniques and it's not always clear who is selling technology and data to whom. Use more than one, and integrate your findings with sites listed in the next chapter under company research.

These sites can be great when you are looking for someone, though I personally find their ability to pull up data a little scary . . . and it probably won't be long before data from Facebook and Twitter starts being integrated, making it scarier still. I worry about the world we are becoming, when everything about everyone is stored on thousands of computers around the world, and privacy is as rare as noble motives.

PeopleData
www.peopledata.com/
There are a number of websites like PeopleData; essentially, they are phone book databases, often with hooks into other databases, such as Intelius, ZabaSearch and ZoomInfo (see the following entries). This allows it to pull up birth dates, names of relatives, and so forth. Like many of these sites, it's a heck of a resource when you are trying to find someone.

ZabaSearch

www.zabasearch.com

This slightly scary website provides free address and contact information for names entered, at no charge. ZabaSearch does not use telephone-
centric resources to look for people; nor does it do web scans like ZoomInfo.
Rather, it uses "public records" (see Intelius, below, for examples of what
that means).

US Search

www.ussearch.com

Another people finder, very similar to Intelius.

Intelius

www.intelius.com

Similar to ZabaSearch, Intelius' data comes from "utility records, court
records, county records, change of address records, property records, business records, and other public and publicly available information." Even
pulls up relatives and former spouses. More detailed information is available for a price; usually not worth it.

Zoom Info

www.zoominfo.com/

Pulling data from a number of resources, this site can come up with sur-
prising results. Although the site wants you to sign up for their premium
services, the free searches are still pretty good. They are building a good
company database.

SearchSystems

http://publicrecords.searchsystems.net/

Another of the public records sites, for finding people and researching their
backgrounds.

Email Lookup

www.email-lookup.com/

This website claims to find people's email addresses. I have not found sites
like this to work very well, but I remain ever hopeful. This site also has
standard reverse-number lookups, even a reverse address lookup (address
in, name out).

YouTube and Other Video Sites
www.reelseo.com/list-video-sharing-websites/

When you're researching someone, you can't afford to overlook social networking and video. Go to such sites, search by the person's name, present and past places of employment . . . whatever comes to mind. You never know what might come up.

Though 90% of videos will be on YouTube, people do use other sites for video as well (hundreds, in fact) and most of them are listed at this website address.

Another Kind of Networking: The Job Club

Here's an interesting little tidbit: one of the most successful ways of finding a job is by picking up the phone book, calling around to the businesses listed in the fields you are interested in, and asking if they have any job openings. This method of job-hunting is listed as having a 69% success rate (meaning that, out of a hundred people who use *only* this method in their job-hunt, 69 of them will be successful). Now, this is the interesting part: if you do *exactly* the same thing, but you do it as part of a group of people who are all job-hunting this way, the rate of success jumps to 84%.

There are a number of reasons for this higher success rate: increased support from those around you; a healthy sense of shame when you're not working your job-hunt as hard as you think everyone else is. And probably most important is the networking side of it. People in the group talk, and they tell each other what they each have found. You may not have had any luck today, but you were talking to an acquaintance who happened to mention that he's looking for someone in the same line of work as Bob, who is sitting over there near the end of the table. And of course, Bob doesn't have anything that can help you right now, but sitting across from Bob is Mary, and Mary just talked to a guy who knows a couple of companies that might be interested in someone like you. And so on. Had these people *not* been getting together with each other, their likelihood of job-hunting success would be the same as if they all had been doing it alone.

Job clubs and similar organizations exist all over the country. Most are free; often, they will have guest speakers and other resources that can help you greatly in your job-hunt. And every other person in the room is usually happy to help you. How often does that happen?

Job-Hunt—Networking Resources by State
www.job-hunt.org/job-search-networking/job-search-networking.shtml
One of the best pages on Susan Joyce's most excellent site. Choose the state you are interested in, and you will find links to job clubs and other resources, both for networking and for job-hunting in general.

And Try These Search Terms
(name of city or area) job club   *job club*

OMG! Texting

Recently, college students and new graduates were surveyed regarding their thoughts on texting, using a typical cell phone. Here are some of the results:

- 11% think it's appropriate to ask for a raise via text
- 32% say it's okay to "call in sick" to work via text (22% have actually done it)
- 11% think it's acceptable to quit a job via text

It gets better. When the same questions were put to kids in the 13 to 17 age group:

- 18% think it's appropriate to ask for a raise via text
- 51% think it's okay to "call in sick" to work via text
- 20% think it's appropriate to quit a job via text

When I saw this, the first word that came to my mind was *clueless*. Texting is fine for letting your spouse know you'll be home late, or letting some friends know that you'll meet them for dinner at 7:00. But texting is not suitable for communicating with a potential employer.

Like email, texting lacks tone. As I've mentioned throughout this book, human communication is complex and multilayered. When dealing with people you know well, they are often able to "read between the lines" of your written communications, using what they know about you to help supply the missing tone—and even then, we have to use emoticons and "LOL" to make sure we are not misread. Common methods of expression, like irony, sarcasm, humor, sincerity, embarrassment . . . none of this comes through in a few typed lines.

The world of business is more about formality than familiarity. And though company cultures do vary, you are more likely to be criticized for texting during your job hunt than for falling to. Play it safe and don't.

Here's more on the survey:

www.secretsofthejobhunt.com/profiles/blogs/texting-and-work-among-the

And here are some articles on the subject:

Why Texting and Job-hunting Don't Mix
http://www.examiner.com/examiner/x-13521-SF-Workplace-Communication-Examiner-y2009m6d21-Why-texting-and-job-hunting-dont-mix

Thx for the IView! I Wud ♥ to Work 4 U!! ;)
http://online.wsj.com/article/SB121729233758791783.html

Mind Your Texting Manners: Are Using Text Messages Okay on the Job Search?
http://blog.employmentguide.com/posts/view/288

Job Search No Place for Emoticons and Texting
http://www.careerbuilder.com/Article/CB-1149-Job-Search-Job-Search-No-Place-for-Emoticons-and-Texting/?ArticleID=1149

However, receiving job leads by text is a different story:

Jolly Saint Nick Spotted Text Messaging Job Leads from iPhone
http://newjobsdb.com/a798720-jolly-saint-nick-spotted-text-messaging.cfm

Employrium Launches Real Tweets Linking Social Media with Job Search
http://jobsmonitoring.com/a778068-employrium-launches-real-tweets-linking-social.cfm

Online Communication: Email

During your job-hunt, you will find yourself registering with quite a few new sites: job boards, blog sites, networking sites, and so on. Every one of them will require your email address to complete such a registration, and often a confirmatory email will be sent to verify that you're a real person. And, sadly, some of the sites you register with will sell your email address—count on it. When you post your resume online, spammer bots will pick up your email address from it. There's no way around it—when you use the Internet in your job-hunt, the level of spam and junk in your email inbox will soar to heights unimagined.

For this and other reasons, I strongly recommend that you get at least one special email address, to be used only for your job-hunt. It will stop your regular, personal email from getting swamped with new spam, and it will help you stay organized during the job-hunt. If you like, you can set it up so the address tells people instantly who you are:

robert.shelton.civil.engineer@hotmail.com
john.sullivan.jobhunter@gmail.com

At any rate, make sure that your email address sounds like business and not like play. If you don't get an email address you like from your personal website host, there are a number of sites that offer free email. The three most popular:

Gmail
http://www.gmail.com/

Yahoo! Mail
http://mail.yahoo.com

Hotmail
http://www.hotmail.com/

Most readers of this book will be well-acquainted with email, having used it for years. A few will be coming to the Internet more reluctantly, and with less experience. It's not my place to teach you the basics of the Internet and online etiquette, but let me mention just a few points:

- When you are job-hunting online, the primary impression that people have of you is from your emails with them. If you dash off quick notes with sentence fragments, spelling errors, and poor grammar, you may never get the chance to make an impression on them in person. Use email as a way of getting your communication to a person quickly, but don't let that sense of speed and efficiency slop over into the way you write.

- When sending email, send it as plain text; don't send emails with HTML formatting, fancy fonts, colored text. The person receiving your email may not be using the same email program as you, may not have the same features, or may have their options set differently. As a consequence, your emails may look like gibberish when received.

- If you must send formatted text, send it as an attachment to an email, using a standard word processing program like Microsoft Word, or an Acrobat PDF (though don't send email attachments unless they are requested). Always explain in the body of the email what the attachment is.

- Make sure the subject line is short, pithy, and accurate. It doesn't hurt to repeat the subject line as an "re:" at the top of the email text.

- Many people have their email clients set up so that a footer is added automatically to every email sent. Most just contain contact information; others may contain aphorisms or statements of philosophy or viewpoint; some of these can get kind of personal and preachy. If you have anything beyond contact information in a footer, turn it off during your job-hunt. Send yourself an email now and then to make sure people are receiving all you think they are, and nothing more.

These links may help you use email more efficiently:

Harness Email
www.learnthenet.com/learn-email/
All about email.

Email Netiquette
www.library.yale.edu/training/netiquette/
From Yale University's library; short but very good. A must-read for every job-hunter.

Email Etiquette
www.emailreplies.com/
Though written as a set of rules for formulating email replies to customers, most of it applies to all email communications.

The Most Important Part of Your Job-Hunt

The most important thing you can do during your job-hunt is sending thank-you notes. Whenever someone does something for you, goes out of their way, or gives you a hand, you should acknowledge them for it. A thank-you note is useless if it isn't prompt, so when someone helps you out, email them a thank-you note within twenty-four hours. In addition, consider sending them another thank-you note by regular mail, through the US Post Office, as soon as possible. There have been many, many times when a simple thank-you note is what made the difference for someone's job-hunt.

Chapter 6

RESEARCH

YOU'RE IN COMPETITION with millions of other people who are looking for a job right now. That company you want to work at? That listing you liked on the job board? You have to think of it as if it's *your job*. Do you want someone else to end up with *your job*? Does that seem fair to you?

Well, even though it's your job, you're not the only one who wants it. There are probably hundreds of people, just as qualified, who want to take that job away from you. So either you're going to have to sit down and wait until life is fair, or you're going to have to work a little harder than everyone else. The main difference between the successful job-hunter, and the somebody-else-has-my-job job-hunter, is *research*. And, as the salary level rises, as the required experience and skill level of the applicant goes up, as the responsibility inherent in the prospective job increases, so does the amount of job-hunting research required.

Luckily, research is one of those tasks for which the Internet was born. It's a worldwide library at your fingertips, which you can access anytime, day or night, without ever leaving your home. A researcher's dream.

But you must do your research with care and intelligence. Too much information is just as bad as no information, and there's so much available that you can be easily overwhelmed.

To address this issue, special types of websites have been created whose primary purpose is to tell you where the data you want is located. Of these, the two you will find most useful are directories and search engines. (There are databases on the web that can also be helpful.)

The saying goes, "browse to learn, search to find." Generally speaking, directories are used for browsing, and search engines are used for finding.

Directories give you a general idea of what's available, and the search engine helps you zero in on the specific data you need.

Directories

Directories are places where you will find links to websites—from a few to thousands—organized by subject. Unlike search engines, where results are determined by software, directories are organized mostly by human hand.

To help with browsing, directories are hierarchically organized by subject. You start with a general heading and move toward more specific groupings. Conversely, a search engine looks for data that will match certain keywords, regardless of subject; but you need to know the keywords to look for. So directories are great for when you need some ideas to help you narrow things down; or when you are looking at general subjects, such as careers, sports, movies, space flight . . . that kind of thing. So even when a directory doesn't have exactly what you are looking for, the subject categories themselves can help you with ideas on keywords to use, if and when you move on to search engines.

Since they are compiled by human hand, the entries in some directories are not as current as you might like; others are meticulously updated. With directories, one size does not fit all. There is a lot of variety among them— just because you didn't find it in one directory does not mean that it isn't in another.

Open Directory Project

www.dmoz.org/

The largest directory on the web, with 4.8 million sites in over a million subject categories. As the "Open" in the name implies, this is an all-volunteer project. Since each entry is examined and reviewed by a real person, and there are about ninety thousand of these real persons involved, there may be some slight bias now and then on the part of the volunteers, who, for the most part, are not professionals. Still, this is the obvious place to start when you are looking for subject information. As an example of the site's depth, check out the Careers page at www.dmoz.org/Business/Employment/Careers.

ipl2

www.ipl.org/

In 2010, the Internet Public Library was merged with the Librarian's Internet Index (both excellent directories) to make a super-directory. Explore a little; under "Resources by Subject," notice the Business & Economics subhead. Here you'll find great links for researching business, trends, even game theory. Also, check out the Associations on the Net page at http://tinyurl .com/285zgke.

Technical Communication Library

http://tc.eserver.org
http://tc.eserver.org/sitemaps
http://tc.eserver.org/sitemaps/categories.lasso
http://tc.eserver.org/about/libraries_that_link.php

This is an unbelievably good site, ostensibly for technical writers, but of course there's much more. This is an example of what some people call the UnderWeb, or the Invisible Web: many resources, over twenty thousand documents, but it's unlikely that much of the content will be returned by search engines. So poke around a little. The first URL listed above is the home page. The second URL points to a page where you can browse (or search) through the subjects; click on one, and the resources under that subject are listed. In this case, a resource could be an article, it could be a list of links, it could be a pointer to other databases like this one. The third URL lets you access the site map as a tag cloud, (see page 67 in chapter 4) and the last URL is a list of other libraries you can go poke around in.

ibiblio

www.ibiblio.org

A digital archive, with connections to many, many thousands of books and websites. Science, literature . . . an amazing breadth of data. Over thirty-three thousand eBooks that you can download, without charge, to your PC, iPad, smart phone, Kindle, and similar devices.

InfoMine

http://infomine.ucr.edu/

Most of the directories listed in this section are general directories. But there are also many specialized directories online; how do we find them? With a *directory* directory, of course.

InfoMine is halfway between a directory and a search engine. When you tender a query, rather than kick back pertinent web pages, it returns resources—databases, libraries, directory sites, and so forth—where you are likely to find the kind of information you are looking for. You can specify the types of resources you want to see. In many cases, you can also browse through the resource types.

Complete Planet
http://aip.completeplanet.com/
Over seventy thousand searchable databases and specialty search engines.

Web Lens
www.weblens.org/invisible.html
Here is a page with links to a variety of resources not generally indexed by search engines.

Online Resources and Databases
http://resources.library.ubc.ca/
From the University of British Columbia, a large collection of databases and other stuff, including resources for researching companies.

Directory of Open Access Journals
http://library.rider.edu/scholarly/rlackie/Invisible/Inv_Web.html
Over two thousand of them.

Educator's Reference Desk Database
www.eduref.org/
A directory with access to a wide variety of subjects and websites.

Yahoo!
http://dir.yahoo.com
One of the best-known sites on the Internet, for many reasons. The Yahoo! directory has a lot of data, but has a more commercial feel to it. Not worthless by any stretch, but not as good as other resources listed in this category.

Google Directory
www.google.com/dirhp
It's not in Google's nature to do anything badly; they don't.

Databases

There is a huge amount of information available in databases on the web, yet much of it is not indexed by search engines. Most databases have a suitable interface that allows you access to their data, but the real problem is how do you find the databases?

Many of the directories listed in this chapter will point you to databases. You can also try adding the words "database" or "archive" to any search engine inquiry (for example, "professional association AND database"). Even when the search engines haven't indexed the information that the databases contain, the engines usually know where the databases are located.

You can also try URL mining. When you find a URL with a question mark in it, that question mark usually means that there is a search of some kind buried in the URL. What are they searching? Usually a database of some kind. So erase everything in the URL from the question mark to the URL's end, then hit the Enter key. Occasionally you will turn up a database, or a link to one.

Furthermore, databases are often linked to each other. When you find a database, put the "link" command before its address, and plug that into a search engine. Syntax varies from one engine to another, but it will usually be something like:

link: http://www.somedatabase.com

This command returns every website that links to the one in the search term. So if any databases link to the site in your search term, this will turn them up.

Search

Constantly growing and changing, the Internet is like a library with no card index, no titles on the book spines, and no head librarian. No one knows everything that is there at any given moment. Directories only know what a person has found and entered into them; and it's impossible for a directory to keep up with the net's rapid and constant change. So when directories are insufficient, we need a different tool—namely, the search engine.

There are a number of search engines online. To understand how to use search engines most efficiently, and to choose the best one for the job at hand, we should look at some specifics about how search engines do what they do. As you know from chapter 2, a search engine works in two stages. Behind the scenes, where we can't see, a software-program spider cruises around the web, looking for certain websites. The spider finds new sites by following links from others.

At this point, things depend on whether it is a general search engine, like Google, or a specialized search engine. The general search engines send their spiders everywhere, building a database of pretty much everything it finds and where it finds it.

A specialized search engine, however, is only looking for specific, limited data, like recipes, or job listings, so it may only go to recipe or job sites.

It's important to bear in mind is that there is always variation in the search engine databases. Even general search engines don't all go to the same websites; and a general search engine may be told to ignore some of the data that it finds. Storing data is expensive, so an engine may be told not to index phone numbers, or tweets on Twitter, or certain databases. But another search engine may have a contract to index tweets, or have a bigger budget for storage. The practical effect of this is that even general search engines can have very different databases, and the specialized search engines certainly do.

Now comes stage two. A customer goes to the search engine website, and enters a keyword or search term. The search engine looks through its database for matches, and returns what it thinks the user wants to see. Notice, now: it doesn't return what's on the web, it returns what's in its database, its particular index of the web. Moreover, each search engine has slightly different rules for what it returns, and the order to put it in (called *ranking*). In 99% of searches, people never look past the first page of search results, so the way that the ranking is done is extremely important. And of course, Internet search is a lucrative business, so the first few results will be *sponsored* results, meaning they're not necessarily what you were looking for, but hey, they're pretty close, and the search site gets good money to put them at the top of the page. It's usually clear which results are sponsored, though this used to be a problem.

From here, it gets complicated. Some search engines sell their databases to other search engines. Some search engines sell their technology for searching a database and ranking the data. Some sell both; for example, a search on Yahoo! uses the database and technology from Bing.

The reason why it's important to know this stuff is because some search engines are better for finding certain types of information than others.

When you are doing some research on the US Government, should you use Google or GovSearch? Searching for Arizona nursing homes . . . Bing or HospitalLink?

Using Search

There is far more to using search engines effectively than just typing in the first words that come to mind. Learning search engine commands, Boolean logic terms, and the proper use of keywords will allow you to use search engines far more effectively. Even clicking where it says "Advanced Search" can be an eye-opener.

As I've said, one of the key differences among search engines is how they rank and order the data from your search query—you *did* want the most relevant results first, rather than buried here and there in a thousand pages of URLs, right? This is the secret sauce of the search engine field, and it affects the quality of your search results. Your ability to phrase your queries correctly also makes a difference. To this end, I direct you to a few places where you can learn more about using search engines and their language:

University of South Carolina—Basic Search Tips
www.sc.edu/beaufort/library/pages/bones/lesson7.shtml
A quick intro on how to formulate search queries. There are links to finding more in-depth information, if you like.

Web Searching Tutorial
www.askscott.com/tindex.html
Easy to understand, yet very complete.

Search Engine Showdown
www.searchengineshowdown.com/
This website keeps its pulse on the search industry (and, yes, it is an industry; the aggregate profits are huge). Has many tips for search engine selection and use.

Search Engine Watch
http://searchenginewatch.com
This site is all about search engines. Very current, though a bit industry-centric for most people.

Search Engines

Google

www.google.com

Years ago, in early editions of this book, I spent a lot of time trying to talk people into using Google for their searches. They were the little guys, going up against big bad Yahoo!, which dominated the search engine industry at the time.

Well, now Google has come to completely dominate every other search engine in sight, and they are even starting to have just the tiniest whiff of 800-pound gorilla themselves, not unlike what Microsoft exuded for so long.

But you can't knock success, and their success is well deserved. Their domination of the industry bothers me, and yet, for general search, Google just plain works best. Even when away from your computer, you can text your queries, or speak them using an Android or iPhone. Patent searches, translation services, Google Docs, Google Earth, Google Maps with street views, and all of the neat stuff in Google Labs. 800-pound gorilla or not, they're hard to resist.

Bing

www.bing.com/

Bing is Microsoft's entry in the search arena. Yahoo! search no longer exists independently; when you use Yahoo!'s search engine, you're using Bing. The search engine that was formerly Jeeves, then Ask Jeeves, then Ask, has thrown in the towel, saying they couldn't compete any longer, either. It's not that I like Bing more than Google, but we should use it every once in a while. It's important that no single company have 100% market share.

Quintura

www.quintura.com/

Most search engines return results in an ordered list, but there are other ways. Quintura takes an interesting approach, returning results in a tag cloud, as mentioned back in chapter 4. By clicking on words in the tag cloud, you can refine your search focus.

Dogpile

www.dogpile.com

Dogpile is one of the metasearch engines, where your query is submitted to a number of search engines, then a few of the returns from each are combined into a list of results. Unfortunately, Dogpile is currently at the effect of some industry turmoil; many of its sources have died, and from what's currently listed on the site, the only search engines left for it to query are Google and Bing. Not a lot of variety there, hmmm? But the Internet is built on change, so check it out and see what it's like when you read this.

Beaucoup
www.beaucoup.com

Beaucoup is a cross between a search engine and a directory. It's likely to bring up different stuff than you're getting from other search sites, though possibly with less depth and breadth. Valuable all the same.

Anoox
www.anoox.com/

They won't say it out loud, but the folks at Anoox see their site's role as the anti-Google. Sort of a cross between a search engine and a wiki, they want their rankings to come from user suggestions, rather than page links and the other auto-criteria used by search engines.

Treehoo!
www.treehoo.com/

I have no idea if it's any good as a search engine, but half their profits go toward planting trees, and I'm trying to atone for driving an SUV. As far as being a useful search engine, we'll see how it does over time.

Blogdigger
www.blogdigger.com/

This is a blog search engine. If you write your own blogs, submit them to the site to be included in its database.

Search Engine Directories

Often, someone will float the idea for a new search engine, put it up on a website for a while, and when it doesn't make everyone at Google quit their jobs in frustration, the site shuts down. Our only countermove is to go to sites like these, which tell us where the neat new search engines are.

Search Engine Guide
www.searchengineguide.com/searchengines.html

A directory of search engines and directories.

Specialty Search Engines

http://searchenginewatch.com/2156351
From Search Engine Watch.

100 Alternative Search Engines

www.readwriteweb.com/archives/top_100_alt_search_engines_april07.php
The list is from 2007, so a number will have already died, merged, or been bought up by larger brethren. Still, an interesting list.

And an Update with 32 More:

www.readwriteweb.com/archives/the_top_100_alt_search_engines_april07_update.php

Researching Industries

We turn now from the tools of research to the job-hunting research itself, which often starts with researching the fields and industries that interest you. You'll want to get industry news, discover trends, professional pay scales, names of associations in the field, schedules of meetings or networking events, and so on. Professional organizations, in particular, can be extremely helpful. Try these:

CEO Express

www.ceoexpress.com/
Links to all kinds of business resources: the financial and business industry press, international business, trade associations . . . lots of stuff here.

Weddle's Professional Associations

www.weddles.com/associations/index.htm
An excellent list of professional associations, from the site of one of the masters of the job-hunt and the web.

Yahoo! Professional Organizations

http://dir.yahoo.com/Business_and_Economy/organizations/professional
A good way to find out more about a particular field is to go to its association, or professional organization. Many such are listed here.

The Center for Associated Leadership—Association Gateway
www.asaecenter.org/Community/Directories/AssociationSearch.cfm
This allows you to search for various industry associations, by name, industry, geographic area, or association type.

Associations on the Net
www.ipl.org/IPLBrowse/GetSubject?vid=13&cid=7&tid=0&parent=0
From the IPL2 directory.

Industry Portals
www.virtualpet.com/industry/mfg/mfg.htm
A terrific page, with hundreds of links. Also, check out their page at www.virtualpet.com/industry/howto/search.htm

Harvard Business School
www.library.hbs.edu/guides/
Research guides at the Baker Library for researching industries.

Thomas Global Register—Industry and Professional Organizations
www.tgrnet.com/main/links.asp
At this page on the Thomas Global Register site, you will find an extensive list of trade and professional organizations.

FedStats
www.fedstats.gov/
A site with links to all kinds of statistics and statistical sources.

Finding Companies

There are a number of ways to go about finding companies: professional associations, LinkedIn, job board directories . . . the list goes on. One of the first places you should go when looking for organizations in your area is your kitchen, or office, or wherever you keep the yellow pages. Online, there are some yellow pages-type websites, but they are never as good as that book sitting in your lap.

Online, there are many resources for finding companies. And more and more, companies are putting their job openings on their websites; even a CEO can figure out that if you don't find the company, you don't find the job.

When nothing obvious is pointing toward the companies you seek, one approach is to use Google to target data on industries and companies.

For example, if you want to find a list of hospitals in Texas, you could go to Google and try this command:

hospitals texas (or texas hospitals)

and you'll get a list of links to pages that list every hospital in Texas. It also works, of course, with Idaho, West Virginia, and Bermuda; and you can replace "hospital" with "waste treatment center," or "accounting firms," or what have you. Occasionally, you may have to tweak the command slightly, perhaps by adding the word "list" or "database" using the appropriate syntax.

As you do these searches, you will encounter many databases and directories. These are extremely useful; make notes about the ones you find. Then, when you are researching particular companies or institutions, go back to the sites you noted and use the "site" command.

For example, one of the hospital directories I found is Hospital Soup, which is primarily a medical jobs database. If I wanted to find the military hospitals in their database, I could use the "site" command along with their URL and the word "military," like this:

site: www.hospitalsoup.com/military

This limits the search to the Hospital Soup website, and returns every entry in their database that has "military" in its name. A simple example, sure, but it shows you how easy it is to focus your research efforts and save a lot of time.

You'll also find companies by looking at the job boards and seeing who is listing jobs there. Moreover, a number of job boards have directories of companies. The descriptions there will sometimes be a bit self-serving on the company's part; but researching the company yourself will balance that out (see Researching Companies on page 135).

Aside from the resources listed here, use your imagination. You'll hit some dead ends, but stick with it, be methodical, and most of all, take lots of notes.

Addresses.com

www.addresses.com/

There are lots of sites like this online. In addition to finding people and businesses, there are reverse email and phone lookups, links to public records, and so on.

Yellow.com

www.yellow.com

Typical of the phone book-type sites on the web.

Vault

www.vault.com/wps/portal/na/companies

A good site for locating companies; you can search using various parameters such as industry, city and state (and country), number of employees, and annual revenue. Lots more at the site as well. Vault is also great for researching the companies you find—see the pages listed in the next section.

Company Database.org

http://companydatabase.org/

Database of companies; one helpful feature is where company profiles show other companies the one in question is affiliated with.

Entry Level Employers' Search

www.collegegrad.com/topemployers/2010_entry_level.php

From the CollegeGrad website, this is a list of employers looking for entry-level employees. If necessary, change the year in the site's URL. There are lots of other tools on the site for researching industries and businesses, so check it out.

Zoom Info

www.zoominfo.com/

This site, long known for finding people, is building a company database as well.

Yahoo! Company Directories

http://dir.yahoo.com/Business_and_Economy/Directories/Companies

A large directory, organized by industry—thousands of companies with links to their home pages.

ThomasNet

www.thomasnet.com/browsecategories

This is the website of the *Thomas Register,* the manufacturer's bible. On this page, you may browse through many thousands of companies, here indexed by category. Be sure and poke around the website . . . lots of stuff there.

100 Best Companies to Work For

http://money.cnn.com/magazines/fortune/bestcompanies/2009/index.html

On the CNNMoney.com website, there is a page with information on which companies are best, according to different criteria. The page here is from their 2009 survey; at the site, you can change the year to something more recent, or look at a number of years to see trends.

Academic 360

www.academic360.com/

Links to over three thousand academic institutions.

Banksite Directory

www.bankdirectory.net/

Links to over seven thousand bank websites.

US Hospital Info

www.ushospital.info/

Links to hospitals and medical centers in the United States.

Hospital Soup Facility Finder

www.hospitalsoup.com/listing/medical-search/

The hospital search page at Hospital Soup.

Restaurant Guide

www.sourceguides.com/restaurants/index.html

For those in the food industry, a database of over 50,000 restaurants organized by state and service type.

Get That Gig—Entry-Level Careers

www.getthatgig.com/

Click on one of many categories, receive a list of employers in that industry looking for entry-level employees.

Researching Companies

When you are researching a company, what do you want to know? The safe answer is *everything*. Once you've targeted a company, there's no such thing as learning too much. But as you start out, the information you'll most want to know comes down to three categories:

Goals and challenges: It's important to know what the company wants to do, so that you can explain to them (and yourself) how you would fit in. How can you help them reach their goals? How will your skills help the company to meet its challenges?

Culture: What kind of a workplace is it, laid back or button-down corporate? Are casual Fridays a big thing, or do people regularly dress in T-shirts and tennis shoes? Does the company talk about eight-hour days but expect you to work twelve? This is the kind of stuff you want to know before accepting any offers.

Questions: When you can anticipate the questions you'll be asked in your interviews and have answers ready, it tells the interviewer that you've done your research, making you a more desirable candidate. Also, you'll want to have a good idea of the answers to your own questions as well. If the answers you get at an interview don't match what your research has revealed, that may indicate a problem.

Everything you can find out is valuable. Are they launching a new product? Are they financially wobbly? Is downsizing on the horizon? Closing or opening branch offices?

The resources listed in this section will help you find out much that you want to know, but use your imagination, too. Read the company's annual report, call the marketing department and find out what they're doing—any new products that might require expanding the employee base? You should also be talking to people, calling your contacts, seeing what your network can do. Try to talk to someone who recently left, or even better, retired from the company. Talk to people who work for the competition, and ask about the firm you're researching. It won't be long before you hear "They're a great company, but . . ." and perhaps you can find out what problems the company has that you can solve. Nobody knows more about Ford's strengths and flaws than Chevy.

Other sources to check out (for publicly traded companies, at least) are the self-trader websites like Scottrade, E*Trade, or Ameritrade.

If you really want to be thorough, then don't forget to use a search engine to search on the company name—don't stop after one page of results. And try search terms using the company name together with words like "harassment," "lawsuit," "scandal," "bankruptcy," "scam," "disgraced, . . ." you get the idea. Check local newspapers as well as doing general web searches.

Finally, visit job boards. Many maintain company databases, some better than others. Check around and see what you find.

Company Research Guide—Rutgers University
www.libraries.rutgers.edu/rul/rr_gateway/research_guides/busi/company.shtml
An excellent guide to researching companies online.

Biographical Resources
http://libguides.rutgers.edu/biographies
Information and links for finding out more about people in business.

Chambers of Commerce
www.2chambers.com/
A directory of state and local Chambers. They will have lots of data on local business; that's their job.

Bizjournals
www.bizjournals.com/
This site gathers together publications from the business press from all over the country. You can search the archive for any mention of the company (or industry or person) that you are interested in; there's a lot here. Access is free. There are other "goodies" on this site as well.

Newslink
http://newslink.org/mbiz.html
Links to a number of business magazines. Also on the site are pages with newspapers, radio and television stations, news services, journalism organizations, and so forth.

Vault Employer Ratings
www.vault.com/wps/portal/usa/companies
Vault's list of best companies, in various categories. Good page.
www.vault.com/wps/portal/usa/companies/layofftrack?sort_by=updated+desc
This is the page where Vault keeps track of companies it knows are hiring, and those that are downsizing.

Direct Employers Association—Member Companies

http://www.directemployers.org/about/member-companies/

This is a list of companies that are members of the Direct Employers Association, who list jobs with Job Central. If you click on a company name, you're taken to a list of their current job listings; ignore them. What you want is the box on the right, under the company name. You can get information on where their branch offices are, what job titles they currently are hiring for and lots of other good stuff.

LinkedIn

www.linkedin.com/companies

This is the page for LinkedIn's extensive company database.

Newslink—Newspapers

www.newslink.org/news.html

This is the Newslink page that will take you to newspapers all over the country, the world, even other planets. Perhaps I exaggerate.

You might be amazed at how much industry and company information you can get from the local newspaper. Search engines do not index every word of every newspaper—far from it. You should go to the newspaper sites themselves to find data.

All You Can Read

www.allyoucanread.com/

Newspapers and magazines—over twenty-two thousand of them, for now—from everywhere.

NewsVoyager

www.newspaperlinks.com/voyager.cfm

Yet another site to find newspapers The accent here is on getting to even the smallest local newspaper.

Annual Report Resource Center

www.irin.com/tf/IRIN/home?path=/cgi-bin/main.cgi&host=www.irin.com&

Annual reports, facts, press releases.

Stock Market Yellow Pages

www.stockmarketyellowpages.com/

A very good page, containing great links to more information, and actually brags about being free . . . kind of refreshing for this category, where so many websites are aiming for the big bucks.

Business Directory—Chambers of Commerce.com

www.chamberofcommerce.com/

This site is a little more than it sounds at first; it is a huge database of businesses across the country.

Free Annual Reports—The Public Register

www.prars.com/index.php

Cool site, has what it says.

Forbes—America's Largest Private Companies

www.forbes.com/2008/11/03/largest-private-companies-biz-privates08-cx_
sr_1103private_land.html

It's actually a better idea for job-hunters to target smaller companies, but I never found *that* website.

INC.'s 5000

www.inc.com/inc5000/list

Inc's list of the five thousand fastest growing companies, with links to more data on each. All kinds of other company lists on the site too: Top 10 by revenue, Top 10 by growth rate, Top 10 Job creators . . . like that.

Securities and Exchange Commission

www.sec.gov/
www.sec.gov/edgar.shtml

All public corporations, domestic and foreign, who do business in the United States are required to file an amazing variety of forms and papers with the SEC. All such filings, and more, end up in the SEC's EDGAR database (which stands for Electronic Data Gathering, Analysis, and Retrieval). EDGAR is huge and it can take a little while to get the hang of using it effectively, but what a tremendous resource. Note the tutorial and overview at www.sec.gov/investor/pubs/edgarguide.htm.

Canadian Business Resource

www.cbr.ca/

Corporate and executive profiles for companies in Canada.

SEDAR

www.sedar.com

The Canadian equivalent of EDGAR, this is a database of filings by publicly traded companies operating on Canadian soil. Also links to basic company profiles.

Allstocks

www.allstocks.com/links/

The Allstocks site has many links to corporate information.

Daily Stocks

www.dailystocks.com/

Lots of stuff here.

Yahoo! Finance

http://biz.yahoo.com/i/

I'm going to just quote the site: "Company profiles from Capital IQ, who provides users with information on over nine thousand public companies, including contact information, business summaries, officer and employee information, sector and industry classifications, business and earnings announcement summaries, and financial statistics and ratios. Yahoo adds stock charts based on historical data from Commodity Systems, Inc. (CSI), and links to other resources." Pretty good.

CEO Express

www.ceoexpress.com/default.asp

On this page are links to a whole bunch of business data. Take a few minutes and check out the amazing possibilities here.

WetFeet Company Profiles

www.wetfeet.com/Employers.aspx

A directory of companies, with profiles with sales data, number of employees, employee turnover rate—ahem, I said *employee turnover rate,* office locations, company and industry overviews, and so on.

4,000 Companies

http://interbiznet.com/hunt/companies/

From Interbiznet, a listing of four thousand company websites that each are supposed to have job listings on the site. Because of the way the Internet changes, many do, some don't. Check it out.

Corporate Information

www.corporateinformation.com/

Although detailed information requires a subscription, this website is a good place to find basic data on thousands of corporations around the world. This includes business description, recent stock performance, annual sales, number of employees, and major competitors.

Researching Private Companies

http://toby.library.ubc.ca/subjects/subjpage2.cfm?id=273

From the University of British Columbia, resources for researching private companies.

Article: The Most Innovative Companies

www.fastcompany.com/magazine/123/the-worlds-most-innovative-companies .html

Fast Company has lots of articles of this sort . . . look around, try different site searches.

Europages

www.europages.com/

Useful for researching European companies and products.

Hoover's Online

www.hoovers.com/

The site doesn't offer as much as it used to, at least not free of charge. As with all of the pay-to-play sites like this, only pay money if the free sites aren't getting you where you need to go.

FINS from The Wall Street Journal
www.fins.com
This is the *Journal*'s latest stab at a jobs website; being fairly new, it will likely morph a bit as it finds its legs. Give it a look; it's rare that the *Wall Street Journal* does anything badly, and the only real question is whether the site content will end up being geared more towards the job-hunter or the employer.

D&B Power Profiles
http://dnb.powerprofiles.com/
Not much depth without buying a membership, but the directory itself is huge; you can browse geographically and see just about every business a town might have.

Peeking Inside

As I promised to keep pointing out, it's not just a company; it's a bunch of people. So when researching companies, you'll want to find out more about the people there. Company reports, news releases, databases and all that stuff helps, but networking and making a few phone calls will usually take you further. To augment your other sources, remember the "Finding People" sources in chapter 5, and try these:

Glass Door
www.glassdoor.com/index.htm
Anonymous ratings from former employees, information about salary, opinions about company culture, and so on. Useful when you can't find a contact at the company, but still want a sense of what is being said around the water cooler.

Spoke
www.spoke.com/
Spoke has a database of companies and people at companies, with profiles of both. They'll want you to join up and pay some money, but if you look toward the bottom of the home page, you'll see where you can look up people and businesses for free. If you give them a name, they'll tell you where he works (if it's in the database), where the company is, how many employees, and so on.

Staff Canteen

www.staffcanteen.com/

Similar in goals to Glass Door, this website is still young, the database incomplete. Some company research is possible here; we'll see what the future brings.

Jobitorial

www.jobitorial.com/

A website where employees anonymously rate the companies they work at.

JobGrades

www.jobgrades.com/

Another site for rating employers.

JobSchmob

www.jobschmob.com/

Another employer rating site, but this one is more of a rant-and-get-out-the-frustration kind of place. My mother often said that there's two sides to every story.

CheckDomain.com

www.betterwhois.com

www.whois.net/

Maybe you don't know anybody at the company you are interested in and you can't seem to come up with a contact there at all, nor do any of the standard business directories help. Assuming the company has a website, you can plug the company's website URL into Network Solution's Whois search engine. It looks through the database of domain registrations and returns basic data about the company, usually including an "administrative contact." If it's a large company, the administrative contact may be the same as the technical contact, which may be just an IT manager or a trusted programmer in the IT department . . . but for smaller companies, you may have just gotten the name and contact information for the head guy, or somebody close to him.

When you get your search results, ignore the message about "This domain is taken"—of *course* it's taken, you knew that. The data you want is farther down.

Looking Deeper

http://domainnamewire.com/2008/11/05/the-poor-man%E2%80%99s-registrant-lookup/

Read this article and get some more ideas about who is associated with a domain name.

Research on Specialized Work and Organizations

Nonprofits, disabled, minorities, part-time, contract...there are many research sources online beyond what I list here. Not only should you try some searches for current information, but out of fifty thousand job boards, many are specialized for minorities, part-time jobs, nonprofits, and so on. These job boards often have lots of support materials, many of high quality. Be sure and check them out. For the most part, I have tried not to list job boards in this research area, either because they are listed in the job boards chapter, or because you are more likely to find them and other resources through standard searches.

Nonprofits and Social Conscience

More Than For-Profits

www.quintcareers.com/volunteering.html

This page, from Quintessential Careers' site, has articles and links to help you research work at various nonprofit organizations around the country.

Nonprofit Jobs

http://nonprofit.about.com/od/nonprofitwork/Do_Good_and_Get_Paid.htm

From About.com, advice and links.

A Professional Advisor's Guide to Working with Nonprofit Organizations

www.pgdc.com/pgdc/article/2004/06/professional-advisors-guide-working-non-profit-organizations

A very informative article.

Careers in Nonprofits
www.bc.edu/offices/careers/careers/careerfields/nonprofits/_jcr_content/
From the website of Boston College, a page with a long list of links related to nonprofit work.

Guidestar NonProfit Database
http://www2.guidestar.org/AdvancedSearch.aspx
Great place to search for nonprofits. Search by name, location, service, and more.

Idealist
www.idealist.org/
This has been a wonderful site for some years. As this book goes to press, they are reorganizing and relaunching, but I expect they will continue their fine work.

National Center for Charitable Statistics
http://nccsdataweb.urban.org/nccsTools.php
Hard data about various nonprofits.

Part-time, Contract, and Temporary Work

The Contract Employee's Handbook
www.cehandbook.com/cehandbook/htmlpages/ceh_main.html
This is an immensely useful handbook, covering every facet of doing temporary or contract work. The site also has a contract employee's newsletter. It's sponsored by the Professional Association of Contract Employees.

Temp Jobs
http://jobsearch.about.com/od/tempjobs/Temporary_Jobs_and_Agencies.htm
From About.com, there are links here to articles about finding temp work, whether it's right for you, and so on.

Directory of Contract Staffing Firms
www.cjhunter.com/dcsf/view_some.html?SearchType=complete
Pretty big list. Find firm names here and research them.

Backdoorjobs.com
www.backdoorjobs.com/

This site (and the book, by Michael Landes, from which the site takes its title) is mostly aimed at young people who are looking for summer situations, temporary jobs, maybe something outdoors, maybe something overseas for a little while. As is typical of this sort of site, the author wants you to buy his book, but even so, there's useful information and news of opportunities online here.

Summerjobs.com
www.summerjobs.com/do/all_employers

This is the employer database at Summerjobs.com. The database is not huge; mostly parks and camps.

Work for Minorities

Job-Hunting after 35
www.stc.org/intercom/PDFs/2002/20020708_20-22.pdf

It's not that the elderly are a minority, exactly; there sure seems to be a lot of them. But if any group is routinely discriminated against in the job-hunt more, with less thought, I don't know who that is. (You might argue African Americans or Hispanics, but try being an *old* African American or Hispanic.) There are not many resources for the elderly when job-hunting, though this article offers the standard advice that is pretty much echoed by everyone else. I was a little upset to find that the keyword *elderly* in a standard Google search kicked back an article about job-hunting after age thirty-five.

Career Resources for Diversity Candidates
www.guidetocareereducation.com/tips-and-tools/diversity

The best resource page on the subject that I have found.

IMDiversity
www.imdiversity.com/EmployerProfiles/

A good database of employers looking to increase their minority hiring.

Work for the Disabled

Getting Hired
www.gettinghired.com/ParticipatingCompanies.aspx
Company database at the Getting Hired job board for people with disabilities.

recruitABILITY
www.recruit-ability.com/
Helping disabled students transition from college to the world of work.

Disability.gov
www.disability.gov/employment/jobs_%26_career_planning
A page with links to work resources for the disabled.

Work Support
www.worksupport.com/
Contains "information, resources, and research about work and disability issues."

Closing the Gap
www.closingthegap.com/index.lasso
A site about the use of information technology to help the disabled in the workplace.

For Ex-Offenders

The United States puts more people in prison per capita than any other country in the world. More than China, more than Russia, North Korea, Iran, or any other country you care to name; in fact, with less than 5% of the world's population, we have almost one-fourth of the world's prison population.

And if we ever decide that some of these people are fit to live among us again, we do almost nothing to help them become useful members of our society.

It is stunning to me how little there is online to help ex-offenders find jobs after release. A better bet may be to look for resources with your local probation department. To the degree you are able, talk to those in your shoes who have had employment success; they will often know what approaches are most successful.

Sadly, most of the websites I have found that cater to the ex-offender population are just trying to sell books, without much more to offer. There are some good books on the subject that I can recommend—my favorites are *No One Is Unemployable,* by Angel and Harney, and *The Ex-Offender's Job-hunting Guide,* by Krannich and Krannich—but actual resources and advice online is amazingly thin.

Ex-Offender Resources and Assistance
www.hirenetwork.org/resource.html
A state-by-state directory of resources for ex-offenders re-entering the world and the job market.

Ex-Offender Re-Entry
www.exoffenderreentry.com/tips.html
This site has a number of links to resources for the ex-offender job-hunter.

Salaries

Whether you are researching industries and fields, or mulling over a specific job offer, you'll want to know as much about the money involved as you can. Your goal, as much as possible, is to find specific salary data for that job *in the city where you will be working.* As you know, salaries vary widely in different parts of the country; make sure you look up cost of living data, which will often explain the wider swings.

Online salary websites have deteriorated markedly over the years, with the commercial temperature now extremely high. You'll often find better salary data through O*Net, Career One Stop, and LinkedIn. And for the best information, nothing beats asking the people who are doing the sort of work you are considering.

JobStar Salary Surveys
www.jobstar.org/tools/salary/sal-surv.cfm
Mary-Ellen Mort, originally a librarian by trade, has built JobStar into one of the better portals on the Internet. Unfortunately, her funding is such that much of her information is limited to California; this is not true of her salary section, which is, hands down, the best I have found online. So before you choose a career, before you hunt for a job, before you go in for the hiring interview, before you start sixth grade, check out what she has on the site.

Job Search Intelligence

www.jobsearchintelligence.com/

The most painless of the salary-centric sites.

The Real Rate Survey

www.realrates.com/survey.htm

On this bulletin board, "computer consultants" (rather broadly defined) post what they made on their last job or contract, and where it was. You can search by salary, location, platform, and so on.

Payscale

www.payscale.com/

This salary site appears to use their own surveys to provide salary data.

Communities and Relocating

There aren't any rules that say you can only look for work where you are currently living. One of the great things about the Internet is its global reach. Part of researching your next job is researching where you want to live.

City Data

www.city-data.com/

There is no site on the Internet that has more city data than this site. Period. For example, it doesn't just tell you the population; it breaks it down by income, gender, race, ancestry, percent of foreign born, level of education, marital status, daytime population change due to commuting, income distribution, unemployment rate, sex offenders (with links to all of their names and addresses), most common occupations for male and female residents, where the hospitals, churches, and schools are . . . and that's just getting started. If you are researching a place to live, you have to go to this site.

Jobmaps

http://jobmaps.us/

Jobmaps is a combination of the Indeed job search engine and Google Maps. Input a job title and a city or state (also works with "US" for the entire country) and you'll get a map showing where Indeed's listings for that job title are located.

The Best Places to Live in America

http://money.cnn.com/magazines/moneymag/bplive/2010/

Want to move to a new city, town, or country place? Wonder which one is best for you? *Money* magazine's site, here, has not only the statistics, weather, housing costs, and so on, for more than twelve hundred cities around the United States but also a wonderful interactive feature called "Find Your Best Place." You rank various criteria (population, climate, crime, schools, and so on.) by how important they are to you, and the search engine will tell you which places fit the criteria as you ranked them. You can specify how many cities you are considering and it will give you the answers with data about each place, including a "cost of living comparator" to help you figure out whether you'll be richer or poorer if you move from where you currently are. Good site. Change the year in the URL as required.

US Census Bureau

http://factfinder.census.gov/home/saff/main.html?_lang=en

Well, who knows more about what's going on in the various communities in America than the government? (I mean the government, not the people we elect.) Anyway, this site has an *unbelievable* amount of information. Type in an address and find out more than you thought possible about the town or city, county, people, businesses, housing . . . very current information, too, not just from the well-known decennial (that means every ten years, amaze your friends) census. With all of this data riding on the work the Census Bureau does, it's no wonder they get so testy when you don't send back the forms.

All You Can Read

www.allyoucanread.com/

Newspapers and magazines—over twenty-two thousand of them, for now. You can learn a lot about a place from its newspaper; the smaller the community, the truer that is. Unfortunately, the Internet is damaging newspapers faster than Jayson Blair, so we'll see what the future brings.

Chambers of Commerce Directory

www.2chambers.com/

Need to know more about a city or town? Interested in a business located in that city? Start at the chamber of commerce. This site also has state and local convention and visitor's bureau links.

Cell Phone Coverage

www.cellreception.com/coverage/

You're moving to a new area, and you want to know how the cell phone reception is for the various carriers. This is where companies are rated for certain areas, along with complaints and kudos for various cell companies.

Home Price Records

www.homepricerecords.com/

If you are moving to a new town and considering buying a home, this site, using Google Maps, will tell you what houses have recently sold for in a given area. Pretty cool.

Housing Maps

www.housingmaps.com/

This site gathers rentals, home sales, sublets, and rooms to rent from craigslist and shows where they are located using Google Maps. You can click on an area and get a listing of what is currently available in various price ranges, or choose a price range and see what is available in different areas. A neat use of the technology.

The Weather Channel

www.weather.com/activities/driving

In a review of a previous edition of this book, someone gave me grief for listing this site. But if you want climate information about someplace, who is going to know more than the Weather Channel? Historical climate data, long-range forecasts, climate trends. Plus extras: if you want to go visit the town or city in question, you can get a driving forecast, with road conditions, special circumstances, weather at your destination, most congested roads, and so on.

HomeFair

www.homefair.com

At HomeFair, there are a number of tools for researching communities. For example, say you are moving from a small town to a job in a big city, but you like living in small towns and want to see what other communities near the new job might be to your taste. Use the "Community Calculator" to see what small towns are within commuting distance. The "Moving Calculator" helps you see the difference in taxes, insurance, and other financial factors related to moving. The "Salary Calculator" compares cost-of-living factors. And so on.

Realtor.com

www.realtor.com

Realtor.com has some of the same features, but is more about finding a realtor, looking at home listings, checking out mortgage rates, and the like. You can also find information on moving, researching schools where you are moving to, renting an apartment, and more.

Both HomeFair and Realtor.com are sponsored by the National Association of Realtors. There is a lot of overlap between the sites, but each also has a slightly (maybe more than slightly) different emphasis.

Sigalert

www.sigalert.com

You know those transponders you can get for your car, that allow you to zip through the toll booths and have the toll charged automatically to your credit card? They're also used to track how traffic is moving along certain urban areas around the country. At this site, you can see what commute traffic is like, how fast everyone is moving, what routes are most effective over time, what areas always seem to have accidents. Especially helpful when considering a commuting lifestyle.

Evaluating the Data

I'll remind you that online research can be extremely complex, often frustrating. And finding data is only part of the job; you have to evaluate it. The net has leveled the playing field for everyone from the largest corporations to the smallest con artist. In many cases, the source of the data—whose website it is on, who wrote the email—will tell you a lot about how trustworthy that data is. For cases that are less clear-cut, let's look at, and expand on, the criteria for evaluating data that I listed in chapter 1:

- **Authority:** Who put the information here? Who wrote it? Why?
- **Accuracy:** How much is verifiable? What were the writer's sources?
- **Objectivity:** Why is the material here? Who supports the site? Why do they support the site? How does the information relate to any site advertising?
- **Currency:** How old is the information? Can it be dated at all?
- What does the site look like? Professional? How is the data presented? Free of typos and spelling erorrs?

The best information is that which comes from multiple sources, each confirming the others. But one of the Internet's common problems is that websites copy what is said on other websites, and it can be hard to trace down exactly where information came from. For example, not long ago, I was doing some research, and on a couple of websites, I noticed a quote that sounded oddly familiar. It took me a minute to realize why: the original writer was me.

Chapter 7

JOB BOARDS

WHEN PEOPLE THINK of "job-hunting online," or "Internet job-hunting," what they usually have in mind is the job boards. Something like, "hmmm, I guess I'll post a resume on Monday, interviews Wednesday through Friday, and then spend the weekend mulling over job offers. And taking a nap, of course. This job-hunting stuff is *tiring*."

Well, click your heels three times and wake up, Dorothy. That's not the world we live in. There are over fifty thousand job boards on the Internet, and most of them are a flat out waste of time. Part of the reason we know this is because not one of those fifty thousand publish figures on their effectiveness. Ever. They'll mention how many unique visitors they have, but they will never give you figures about how many end up with a unique job.

Think of it. Companies that don't brag about their product? Imagine the commercials: our aspirin won't cure a headache, but lots of people take it. Our soda tastes awful, but lots of people drink it. Our movie is the worst, but everyone goes to see it anyway, and you should, too.

If you are going to spend any time at the job boards, you should use them *effectively,* which means that you will have to use them *imaginatively.* If you merely post your resume (and wait), or mail off your resume in response to listings that look appealing (and wait), then you are likely to remain unemployed for quite a while (still waiting . . .). Most job boards have up to forty resumes for every job listing—and remember, not all of the job listings represent real jobs. The job listings that are real each receive hundreds of responses. If you use the job boards in this traditional way, the way that the job boards *tell* you to, then you are merely playing a numbers game. The odds may be somewhat better than going down to the corner store and buying a lottery ticket, but the methodology is *exactly* the same.

As I've said, most experts credit the job boards with an effectiveness of between 4% and 10%. Some have calculated the effectiveness as even lower: as low as .4%. Think of it: out of every thousand people that buy our soda, four of them manage to swallow it, while everyone else has to spit it out man, that stuff is *nasty*. For every thousand people that take our aspirin, 996 still have a headache. Rush on down and get yourself some today. (Well . . . maybe wait until you feel better . . . .)

The problem is that the job boards are touted as a complete solution to the I-need-a-job problem. And they are, for four people out of a thousand, or four people out of a hundred, or ten out of a hundred, or whatever the figure is (although nobody mentions over what period of time—a job that comes only after two years of hanging around the job boards is not exactly a *complete* solution) and it's insane for you to behave as if you will be one of the lucky few.

So, then, how does one use the job boards imaginatively? There are two ways. One is to use the job boards as they were intended—post your resume, respond to listings—but limit your time there, and choose which boards you use *very carefully*. The other is to mine the (carefully chosen) job boards for whatever data you can find and use that to learn more, expand your research, target companies to see who is hiring, check what their competitors are doing, and so on.

We already know that the Supersites are the least effective of the job boards; they're just big. So of the remaining job boards, which are best?

RECRUITERS

When recruiters and staffing concerns advertise on job boards, it's pretty rare that they are actually advertising a real, live, sitting-there-waiting-for-you job. If you're lucky, they're trying to build up their client base, so that they can offer one of their employer clients (or clients-to-be) a wide range of potential job candidates. Other times—particularly in the medical field, I don't know why—they want to sign *you* up as a client, which involves you paying the recruiter a fee. ("It's hard to place clients like you, you know; of course, it would be different if you had *just* a couple more years of experience . . .")

And some recruiters or staffing companies will charge you a fee, so they can find a position for you that suits your unique skills. At the same time, they will also charge a fee to the employer, who hired them to find people like you. As I have said throughout the book, spending money should always be low on your list of options.

The answer is, generally speaking, the regionals and the niche boards. As I explained earlier, there is no sense advertising in California for a job in Florida, and if you work in the health field, why look for a job on a board meant for real estate agents? Most of the explosion in the number of job boards has come from such specialized sites.

Caveat Hunter

Another reason for the great increase in the number of job boards is that job boards make money. And unfortunately, some of them make money by taking advantage of the job-hunter. So we should probably look at some of the pitfalls when dealing with job boards.

Few people are as vulnerable as the person who is out of work. Self-esteem issues aside, rarely in our lives do we feel such a mixture of hope and despair weighing on us; seldom do we feel so powerless, so much at the effect of events beyond our ability to control or comprehend. It's hard to believe that anyone would take advantage of someone in this situation.

But people do. One common approach to doing so is the free resume review. I've never heard of a single occasion when a resume, tendered for such an examination, was praised as excellent, great, unable to be improved upon. More often, the same company—often the same *person* that reviewed the resume—will offer to rewrite it for you. Hey, he'll even reduce the normal fee, knowing how strapped you are right now.

Having a resume writer review your resume for you is not unlike asking your insurance beneficiary to check your parachute straps: subsequent events may exceed all of your expectations. So the first thing you should do is avoid dealing with any job board that pressures you to take advantage of such a service. (Offering, of course, is one thing, pressure another.) If you want to have someone review your resume, then find someone with experience as a hiring manager, and see what that person says. If you think your resume might need work, then it's best to hire someone to review it; if changes are recommended, and you choose not to do the work yourself, then hire someone completely separate from the reviewer for the rewrite. (I would also recommend that you find local people to do this work, rather than contracting with someone at a job board.)

Furthermore, on the subject of fees, no job board should charge you, ever, for anything. Don't ever pay to apply for a job. Don't pay for "premium memberships" or pay to see "exclusive listings." Don't fill out any "just in case" job applications, and don't give out your phone or social security numbers.

Do expect that any job board you visit will most likely want you to register. That's okay; but tell them nothing beyond your name, your email address, the general area where you live, and your career field. (Yes, the amount of spam in your email will rocket astronomically; almost everyone on the Internet sells email addresses, nothing to be done about it.) Any job board that claims to need your social security number or other such data is to be avoided, although Federal government sites, during the application process, are an exception.

Here are some articles about the risks of online job boards—read them:

Common Job Board Scams
www.resumark.com/blog/andrews/three-common-job-board-scams/

Online Job Board Horror Stories
www.gradtogreat.com/tips_advice/article-jobboard_scams.php

Job Board Scam Alert
www.bankrate.com/brm/news/advice/scams/jobboards.asp

Read the Comments
http://joblounge.blogspot.com/2008/05/posting-resume-on-ladders.html
The comments that follow this short article are very typical.

Liars At The Ladders
www.asktheheadhunter.com/newsletter/OE20090120.htm

6 Common Job Scams
www.careerbuilder.com/Article/CB-563-Job-Search-Too-Good-to-Be-True-6-Common-Job-Scams/

When Is A Job Board Not A Job Board?
www.whatjobsite.com/When%20is%20a%20job%20board%20not%20a%20job%20board.htm

And Try These Search Terms
job board rip offs	*job board scams*
Jobfox scam	*ladders scam*

Borderline

Over time, it has become obvious to people who run the job boards that the best way to maximize profits is to focus on what the industry calls the "professional/local intersection." This is just another way of saying that both employers and job-hunters prefer the specialized boards, the regionals and the niche sites. Or at least the appearance of specialization.

I want to give you an example of something you will probably run into eventually, the job-board network. There is nothing illegal about it; I can't even say it is unethical. But it can waste a lot of your time, and to the job-hunter, time is more valuable than gold.

What do you do when you are an Internet entrepreneur, and you want to start a new job board? How do you begin? A number of companies will sell you the necessary software; some even sell complete pre-packaged job board websites. But what good is an empty job board? You need job listings to attract job-hunters, so you can talk about "unique visitors," so you can attract more employer job listings, so you can attract more job-hunters . . . you get the idea.

Recently, I visited a job board called Beyond.com. Acting like any out-of-work nurse, I had it do a search for nurse listings in the state of California. It came back with 4,196 listings. Unfortunately, many were work-at-home schemes that had nothing to do with the medical field—not sure how a search on *nurse* turned those up—and quite a few listings were from recruiters and staffing agencies.

It happens that Beyond.com is one of the job boards in what is officially known as the "Beyond.com Network." So I went to another one of the job boards in their network, a well-known site called 4Jobs.com. How many nurse listings in California?

4,196.

Hmmm.

Okay, how many California nurse listings at the network's Career Sites job board? 4,196. Local Gigs? 4,196. Seemed to be the same work-at-home and recruiter listings, too.

Obviously, either these different job boards are all using the same database of job listings, or there are some *pret-ty* funny things going on in California hospitals these days.

Well, let's try some of the niche sites in the Beyond network of job boards. The network is broken down into some extremely fine specialties; between the niche and regional sites, there must be thousands of job boards.

Let's try . . . the Flight Attendant Job Site Just for the heck of it . . . how many California nurse listings?

Fifty. Well, that's a relief in one way, I guess, but are these medically trained flight attendants?

Let's try their hotel and travel industry board, "Hospitality Gigs." How many California nurse job listings?

Fifty.

Seventeen of them are work-at-homes, the rest appear to be recruiters.

How about the "Airport Staffing" job board? How many nurses? (Guess.) "Real Estate Agent Careers"? "Restaurant Manager Job Site"? "Hotel Manager Jobs"?

Same answer. Exact same job listings, down to the scams and the posting dates (almost three months prior . . . maybe it's hard to start an IV when you're talking square feet and new carpeting).

So now we have an answer about what you do when you want to start a job board, but don't have any job listings. You can buy the listings, along with everything else. If you're serious about your job board, then over time, you can get your own flight attendant or real estate agent or hotel manager listings in the database, and you can drop the nurses and other jobs that aren't part of your intended niche . . . *if* you're serious about setting up a true job board. On the other hand, if you keep using listings that don't address the specialized clientele, and you keep setting up more specialty sites with finer and finer hair-splitting distinctions between job titles, then it's possible that you're not really setting up job boards at all. It's far more likely that you're setting up a network of resume-collection sites; you then charge employers to look at the resumes. All of this means, that even without the work-at-home schemes and recruiter listings, looking for a real job at places like this is a waste of your time.

The Beyond Network

www.beyond.com/network/career-communities.asp

Over three thousand job boards on this page, with many regionals and an amazing number of specialty boards.

In fact, some of the job boards are so over-specialized it's ridiculous. Under the Health Care heading, there were 234 separate job boards; IT had 279. My personal favorite job boards are "Child Support Investigator.com", "Environmental Compliance Inspector.com", and "Gaming Change Person .com"—which is a different website from "Gaming Cage Worker.com."

The Gorilla in the Job Board

Basic business theory says advertise to create new customers, service to create repeat customers. Advertising is expensive; service, relatively speaking, is cheap it's just delivering the product. So, as a businessman, if I spend a little money making you my customer, then you'll pay me to stay my customer. And as long as I keep you happy and deliver the product you want, you'll keep paying. That's how I stay in business.

When it comes to the job boards, who is the customer? It ain't you and me, my friend; we're the product. We're not repeat business; after all, job-hunters only come around when they're unemployed. You could almost make an argument that whoever is running the job board doesn't have much interest in whether we get a job or not; in some ways, he's better off if we don't.

The employer is the repeat customer, since he's likely to need multiple employees. You only need one job. So it's the employer who is the real customer, it's the employer that the job board needs to keep happy, and if there is a lot of job-hunter turnover, that's cool. More resumes to sell. Sadly, many job boards focus on exactly this model. But even the best job boards, where people genuinely want to help the job-hunter, are aware that the employer is the one who pays the bills. Best that you always remember that.

So how do you know if a job board is genuine, or just a place to collect resumes? Personal recommendations help, and you can read this article, run the name of the job board at Digg, and see if there's anything about it at Job Board Reviews:

Which Job Boards Have Good Hiring Success Rates?
http://tinyurl.com/46st26p
This article explains a bit about success rates, and how they can be .4% or lower. Also gives some good criteria for choosing job sites.

If it's a niche site, catering to a certain profession, then look in their job listings and see if there are jobs that shouldn't be there, as I did with the nurse jobs on the Beyond Network's niche sites. If it's a regional, then a job board for Atlanta shouldn't be showing any jobs in San Diego. A database of job listings that appears contaminated in this manner usually indicates problems. Work-at-homes and obvious recruiters are also red flags.

Another thing I've noticed is that sub-par job boards tend to have a fairly low Google PageRank score, generally below 5. It's not foolproof, nor does it stand alone; it's just more evidence to weigh.

Digg
http://digg.com/
Digg is a place where people go to talk about their experiences, so often job stuff comes up.

Job Board Reviews
www.jobboardreviews.com/
This slightly schizophrenic site feels very new, and a bit unfocused. Still, I have high hopes for it; see what you think.

Wikipedia—Google Page Rank Explained
http://en.wikipedia.org/wiki/PageRank
It's named after Larry Page, and is central to how Google ranks websites. The early going is easy to understand, but after that it's eigenvectors, stochastic matrices, and your favorite and mine, the Perron-Frobenius theorem.

Google PageRank Checker
www.prchecker.info/check_page_rank.php
Input a web address, this returns the site's PageRank. Pretty neat little tool.

Finding Job Boards

When you go looking for job boards, you generally won't have to look too far. Any search engine will pull up more than you could possibly imagine. So when you search, try and narrow the focus. If you are looking for regionals, then search on "Boston job board" or "Los Angeles jobs." If you are looking for a niche or industry site, search for "aerospace jobs" or "health job board." If you have an employer in mind, then try a search like "IBM jobs" or "tenet hospital jobs." You can also do a search on "top job boards" because there are people who write articles that are similarly titled, and some sites have yearly Top 10 or Top 30 lists. However . . . I am amazed at the boards that end up on those lists, and I strongly suspect that the surveys involved are either poorly designed, or are being gamed. The boards on the lists are closer to "Best Known" than "Best." Besides, are they the top job boards for employers? Recruiters? Job-hunters? Job board owners? Nobody knows. Don't depend on such surveys.

Here are some websites you can use for finding job boards:

Association Job Boards
www.associationjobboards.com/find.cfm
Many industry associations have, or are associated with, job boards that cater to their industry.

Weddle's Directory of Associations
www.weddles.com/associations/index.cfm
Another list of associations, likely to have job boards and similar resources.

The International Association of Employment Websites
www.employmentwebsites.org/website/roster
This is a good-sized list of job boards and similar websites.

JobSpider
www.jobspider.com/job/directory/employment-resources.asp
A directory of employment resources; many of them are job boards.

What to Do with Them

As you know, if you only go to job boards to throw resumes around, you are putting yourself at a disadvantage. The job-hunt leaves you little enough power as it is; don't willingly throw even that small amount away. Once you have found a good job board, instead of just posting your resume or replying to listings, leverage the information you can get out of the site.

For example, don't just run a search on the job titles you are interested in. See what companies are putting up listings in your field, and then run searches on the company names. This will tell you who is doing the most hiring right now. When a company is hiring for a few positions, it usually indicates that they are just dealing with normal turnover. But if they are hiring for a large number of positions, they are expanding, or launching a new product. You've learned how to research and find their competitors; so, how are their competitors responding? Are they hiring as well? If they aren't, should they be? Is there a proposal you should be making to one of the competition?

If a company is hiring for a large number of positions, it may be part of a phased hiring program. Do some research, use your contacts, and find out if this is it, or are there other positions they will be hiring for soon? Perhaps you would be perfect for one of those, and you'd save them the trouble of having to list it on the job board and crawl through the resumes.

What positions are they hiring for? What does that tell you? If an electronics firm is hiring assemblers, then a new product may be on the way, or they may be hiring to fulfill a new contract. What other positions would be required in each case? Sales, shipping, buyers, advertising, HR, secretaries and office assistants, warehouse . . . gather information, make inferences, confirm, modify, refine. Talk with people. Think your way into a job, while your job-hunting competition is sitting around, waiting for their resume to be noticed.

Collection of Job Boards

The following is an eclectic collection of various job boards. Most are good job boards, but of course many good job boards are not listed here. If one of these works for you, or helps to give you ideas, then I am pleased. If one of them does not work for you, or causes you problems, then I am certain it is the fault of my editor. Problems always seem more manageable once blame is assigned.

OUR RESUME COULD USE SOME WORK

You can read more about this online, but there was a bit of a scandal that hit the job board industry a while back. A well-known job board was offering free resume reviews. Those who submitted their resumes would get back a form letter, which would point out flaws in certain sections of their resume. Sometimes, the resume under discussion had no such sections.

Many people paid significant money to have this job board re-write their resumes.

The letters I have seen indicate that in some cases the charge was as little as $650, in others over a thousand dollars.

But the best part is that some of the people who had their resumes written there submitted these same resumes for the free review. And got back the same criticisms, sometimes *from the person who wrote the resume.*

Just when you think people can't surprise you anymore . . .

Dice

www.dice.com

Not that many job boards have excellent reputations; this one does. Significant number and quality of job listings, and an extensive employer directory.

CollegeGrad.com

www.collegegrad.com

An excellent site for recent graduates. Their employer database is well done, and you can see who is hiring, whether a Masters is required, how many hires last year, and so on.

LawJobs

www.lawjobs.com

Good database of legal job listings for attorneys, paralegals, legal secretaries, and the like, the site also includes temp positions and an extensive directory of legal recruiting firms. My experience has been that few legal firms hire directly, at least at the entry level, and recruiters are considered a standard part of the process.

Regional Help Wanted.com

http://regionalhelpwanted.com/corporate/index.cfm
http://regionalhelpwanted.com/corporate/our_sites_usa.cfm

RHW operates about three-hundred fifty job boards around the country. Almost every one is named for the city it is in, followed by "help wanted dot com." (A directory of all sites is at the second URL.) They have high visibility due to their distinctive radio commercials.

craigslist

www.craigslist.org

You can't forget craigslist; it is the local job board that's everywhere. It's less expensive for employers to post here than at most other job sites, so many do. But there is also a higher incidence of scams, identity thefts, and other problems, so just remember to be diligent when looking at any job listings here.

USAJobs

www.usajobs.opm.gov

The official job board for the United States government.

America's Veteran

www.fedshirevets.gov/

There is currently a push to hire disabled veterans for government jobs.

Jobs for PhDs

http://jobs.phds.org/

As job boards go, this one used to be kind of quirky, but is now more mainstream. Listings here tend to focus on academia and research positions.

Senior Job Bank

www.seniorjobbank.org/

A very unusual niche board in that it lists jobs for seniors. Granted, there may not be a huge number of jobs in the database, but it's nice to see that someone is even thinking about this part of the population. The site is associated with another similar site called Work Force 50 (www.workforce50.com/).

HCareers

www.hcareers.com/

A job board for the hospitality industry—primarily hotels and restaurants. You can search by management or non-management positions; it has an employer database.

Just TechJobs

www.justtechjobs.com/

A job board focused on IT jobs. The site has some variations; for example, www.justtechwriterjobs.com is pretty much the same site, same job listings, and so forth.

SnagAJob

www.snagajob.com

Part-time and full-time hourly jobs. Restaurant, retail, convenience store . . . lots of job listings from a long list of quality employers.

Jobs In Recycling

www.jobsinrecycling.net/

Not a huge amount of jobs at the moment, not a dazzling list of employers, but we know size doesn't mean much when it comes to job boards.

Great Green Careers

www.greatgreencareers.com/

Focusing on jobs in energy, environment, skilled trades, and transportation.

Green Job Spider

www.greenjobspider.com/

Affiliated with the previous 2 job boards listed, this is actually a job board search engine that searches only green job boards: recycling, alternative energy, materials, and so on.

Jobvertise

www.jobvertise.com/

An unusual job board, in that they do not necessarily charge either employer or job-hunter. Of course, some cash flow is needed, so employers are offered some premium services, but generally the board seems to be a good idea. It's been around since 1998, so they're doing something right. Resume to listing ratio is about 4 to 1, very low for the industry.

iFreelance

www.ifreelance.com/

Designers and creative people post their profiles, people who need a project completed post their projects. The board brings them together. Neat idea.

Crowdspring

www.crowdspring.com/

Something like the previous listing. Graphic designers (including web and industrial designers) and writers connect to people with projects. At press time, almost eighty thousand designers and writers were registered with the site.

GuruEmployer

www.guru.com/

Similar to the previous two listings, but the Guru board expands the playing field. In addition to creative arts, technology and business jobs and jobseekers are available.

The Write Jobs

www.writejobs.com/

A writer's job board. Maybe I should make a note . . .

Technical Writers Jobs

http://tc.eserver.org/dir/Careers/Job-Listings

Not a job board itself, but a page of links to job boards and websites for technical writers and those in the professional, scientific, and technical communications fields.

EntertainmentCareers.Net

www.entertainmentcareers.net/

A job board for those in film, television, and live theater, listing a wide range of jobs in broadcasting, television news (if you ever doubted that TV news was primarily entertainment, look where they advertise their job openings), production, film studios, theaters, and so on.

Telecommuting Jobs

www.tjobs.com/

This site actually seems to have a good reputation. They do not accept work-at-home schemes, envelope stuffing, and the like. More like freelance jobs that can be done from a home office, like medical transcription.

Getting Hired

www.gettinghired.com/ParticipatingCompanies.aspx

A job board for the disabled.

LatPro

www.latpro.com

The best of the diversity boards, with good resources and a large database.

Net Temps

www.net-temps.com/

One of the top job boards, focusing on temp jobs and staffing.

Volunteering

National Park Service—Volunteering

www.nps.gov/getinvolved/volunteer.htm

This is where the National Park Service posts information about internships, employment, and volunteering opportunities.

Volunteer Canada

http://volunteer.ca/home
http://volunteer.ca/i-want-volunteer/volunteer-centres
This is a government-funded website for volunteering in Canada. More of a clearinghouse for information than an actual place to look for situations. To volunteer, link up with one of the two hundred volunteer centers—okay, *centres*—across Canada at the second URL.

VolunteerMatch

www.volunteermatch.org
A good site for finding volunteer programs in your area. Mentoring, community projects, outreach to the elderly, local library book drives, neighborhood food banks, and so on.

Chapter 8

LAST

The Interview

Your resume is just sales literature. The interview is your sales call, where you are looking to close the deal. To do this, you need to know everything about the company you can; research them completely, online and off. Write down questions that you might be asked, and your answers. Look at your resume, think of your background, and anticipate any questions about your weaknesses. Try to turn any negatives into positives. Don't badmouth past companies or co-workers, and if asked why you left or were terminated, don't tell long, self-serving stories.

There are a number of practice interviews online, but the best thing you can do is have a friend play the role of an interviewer, and practice going through it. Have your spouse sit in. Stop when necessary to work out better ways of answering questions. If you know of anyone who has interviewed at the company you are interested in working for, talk to them. If you know anyone who conducts many job interviews at his work, ask for advice.

Here are some online videos that will instruct you on the on the basics:

Job Interview Questions and Answers
www.youtube.com/watch?v=epcc9X1aS7o

How to Prepare for the Job Interview
http://www.youtube.com/watch?v=0p_A2P_uvzc

How to Communicate Your Strengths
www.youtube.com/watch?v=PapEY2EcoMI&NR=1

Job Interview Tips

www.youtube.com/watch?v=nPbiJTVMdqY

For the first twenty seconds, you're going to think I'm nuts, but listen to what she has to say. If you're not experienced at interviewing, she has some really good points.

And some websites:

Interview Tips: Questions and Answers

www.eduers.com/resume/Job_Interview_Skills.htm

Very good guide.

Job Interview Tips

www.bls.gov/oco/oco20045.htm

From the Occupational Outlook Handbook, one of job-hunting's bibles.

Ask—Job Interview Questions and Answers

http://jobsearch.about.com/od/interviewquestionsanswers/a/interviewquest.htm

One of the best pages in Ask's extensive library of job-hunting data. This page has a long list of possible (and likely) interview questions, with links to the "best" answers.

And Try These Search Terms

But be advised that almost any website that a search engine returns that has the words "job interview" in its URL is more interested in selling you something than in helping you improve your interview skills. Remember the Gateways as well.

job interview questions & answers	*job interview tips*
job interview help	*job interview practice*
YouTube job interview tips	*YouTube job interview help*

Self-Employed and Home Business

Some people are just happier working for themselves, even if the hours are long and the pay is short. Try these sites for more on self-employment:

Free Agent Nation
www.fastcompany.com/magazine/12/freeagent.html
The workplace is changing dramatically. Among these changes is the fact that for some, self-employment has become a broader concept than it was in another age. The concept can now include not only those who own their own business, but also free agents. These are independent contractors who work for several clients; temps and contract employees who work each day through temporary agencies; limited-time-frame workers who work only for a set time, as on a project, then move on to another company; consultants and so on. This is a fascinating article to help you decide if you want to be part of this trend, on the site of the popular magazine *Fast Company*.

Small Business Administration
www.sba.gov
The SBA was established to help start, manage, and grow small businesses. Lots of useful stuff here; also, check out the "Starting a Business" resources at www.sba.gov/smallbusinessplanner/plan/index.html.

Business Owner's Toolkit
www.toolkit.com/small_business_guide/index.aspx
Lots of information here for the small business owner. Everything about your business: starting, planning, financing, marketing, hiring, managing, getting government contracts, taxes . . . all that stuff.

GOVERNMENT JOBS

Almost everything I have been talking about throughout this book could use an asterisk next to it when we start discussing jobs with the Federal government. In fact, jobs at almost every level of government can often be put in a special category. At times you will find that even the way that you apply for such jobs is rigidly set in all sorts of archaic laws and statutes.

And yet, the government is, collectively, the nation's largest employer. It doesn't make sense to ignore jobs with the government just because you have to jump through a few more hoops. But to give you a taste, check out:

How Federal Jobs Are Filled
www.fedshirevets.gov/job/filled/index.aspx

Working Solo

www.workingsolo.com/

Working Solo is a good site for the home or small business worker.

A Home-Based Business Online

www.ahbbo.com

www.ahbbo.com/articles.html

A great site, with lots of information for you if you want to learn about a home-based business. There are dozens of articles at the second URL.

Nolo Law Center for Small Business

www.nolo.com/legal-encyclopedia/

Nolo Press publishes a lot of do-it-yourself law books; this is the part of its website that offers legal resources for the small business person. Really good.

Jobs and Moms—Work at Home

www.jobsandmoms.com/work_at_home/

www.jobsandmoms.com/work-from-home-biz-ideas-for-moms/

Some articles from the Jobs And Moms website.

And Try These Search Terms

self employed	*home business*
work for yourself	*entrepreneur*

However, ignore any website or advertisement that asks for money, or even hints that you could work at home for them. There is nothing that such people are offering that you would want.

Grants

It may be that the work you most want to do right now is not of the sort for which most companies would be willing to pay you. Perhaps you are a writer researching a book, or an artist, sculptor, or musician. Maybe you want to run a social program for the homeless or engage in similar selfless endeavors. For those of you who are drawn to pursuits for which our society does not generally pay well, if at all, I present a list of sites where you can investigate the possibility of a grant.

Now, don't think for a moment that this is easy, or a way to get through life without working, or any kind of substitute for a "real job." The chances of *ever* getting a grant are astronomically small, and it is an area where those who know the most about how to get a grant will generally come before those who are more worthy, but ignorant of the process. And, even if you *do* get the grant you are seeking, you must properly manage the project being funded, account for all money to the penny, and make sure you avoid even the appearance of impropriety. A job is *way* easier.

But people who are drawn to these sorts of things are usually not the types who let little things like extreme difficulty deter them, so here goes:

Grants.gov
www.grants.gov
The federal government gives away millions of dollars every year, and unless your uncle is a US Senator, your only way of getting some of this money is through the competitive grant process. That is, you write and submit a proposal, as do many, many other people, and if your proposal is judged to be one of the more worthy, you receive the money necessary to fund it. Or, more likely, nowhere near enough money to fund it—at least, not from a single source.

GrantsNet—An Electronic Roadmap for Grants
http://dhhs.gov/asfr/ogapa/aboutog/grantsnet.html
This Health And Human Services site lists many of the rules and requirements for getting a government grant.

Database of Arts Resources
www.artsnet.org/databases/
If you are an artist looking for funding, this is probably the first Internet resource you should turn to. Includes an excellent searchable database of funding sources.

National Endowment for the Arts
http://arts.endow.gov
You've heard of these guys, right? So has everyone else.

SRA International

www.srainternational.org/sra03/grantsweb/index.cfm
At the website of the Society of Research Administrators International, there is information on public and private funding sources for those in the research community. There is a lot of information here.

Overwhelmed?

Once you have found a job board that appears to be a good one, you can of course post your resume or check for job listings, as described elsewhere in this book. If you do this at a number of job boards every day, you're going to quickly find that going to each site, logging in, looking around . . . it can be quite a pain, and time consuming besides. Combine this with using Linkup, SimplyHired, and maybe a Twitter job searcher and you may find yourself with the need to streamline how you get this information. Time to learn about Really Simple Syndication, or RSS:

RSS Explained

www.squidoo.com/rss-explained
A terrific article. The examples are about blogging only, but the way it's described works for all feeds.

What Is RSS?

www.whatisrss.com/
More elementary stuff.

Wikipedia—RSS

http://en.wikipedia.org/wiki/RSS
WP's take on it.

Also check into aggregators like Flipboard, for collating social networking data and more.

URL Friend

Remember that instead of typing in the web addresses (URLs) of each website listed in the book, you can just go to the book's companion website and click on the appropriate link, or download a file of such links to your computer.

Job-Hunting Online Companion Website
http://job-huntingonline.webs.com

When this book went to press, every website was accurately represented, and every website that I've talked about was exactly as I described. But this is the Internet, and this company buys that company, this other one goes out of business, this website gets reorganized and pages are moved around . . . so what you find as you read this book may be slightly different than when the book was finalized. And that's okay; world turning, Internet changes. Nobody at your high school reunion was a teenager.

As time passes, I will try and keep up with such changes, and post them on this book's website. It would help me if you could alert me to any problems or changes that you find, by writing to me through the same site.

But I'll grant you that there's few things more frustrating than clicking on a link and coming up with some kind of page error. Sometimes, the website itself will have disappeared, but usually, the page has just been moved to some other location on the site. It's still there . . . somewhere. Here are a few techniques to try:

First, go to your search engine, and as the search term, type the name of the entry I have given you. Let's use this example:

The Dirty Dozen Online Job Search Mistakes
www.job-hunt.org/jobsearchmistakes.shtml

So your search term is "dirty dozen online job search mistakes," although you can also try shorter versions like "dozen job search mistakes" or "dozen job mistakes." Look at the addresses returned; are any of them at the correct website (www.job-hunt.org)? If so, click on that entry, and the correct page will probably come up.

If that doesn't work, then search using the entry's title, just like last time, but follow it with the "site" command, like this:

dozen online job search mistakes site: www.job-hunt.org

This forces Google to only look on the job-hunt website for this article. If you have no success, try more than one search engine.

If you still can't find the right page, the next thing to try is URL chopping. Since URLs are hierarchical in nature, you are trying to make the URL less specific; you chop off the right-most section of the URL, starting from the slash that is nearest the right hand side. Here is an example:

www.thejobspider.com/job/directory/employment-resources.asp

In this case, you would chop off "employment-resources.asp," leaving only

www.thejobspider.com/job/directory/

and press the Enter key. If this results in a good page, then look around for a hyperlink or other reference to the page you want; try using the site's Search function, if one is available.

On the other hand, if you still get a page error, chop off the next right-most section ("directory/"), and so forth. If you get all the way down to just the domain (www.thejobspider.com), and you still are getting an error, a page that makes no sense, or an offer to buy the domain, then chances are that the website has in fact disappeared. Go back to step one, where you were searching on the article or page title, and see if any of the other search returns look helpful. In a pinch, you can sometimes click on the part of the search return where it says "cached," and you'll get a partial picture of what the page used to look like before it went wandering off.

And sometimes you may find that the site, or its data, is not to be had. Ah well; that's the Internet.

In Closing

One of the problems with doing your job-hunt research on the Internet (or writing a book about it) is that you can find so many interesting side paths. It's easy to waste huge amounts of time, all the while being under the illusion that you are hard at work: "Hey, what do you mean I'm not job-hunting enough? I was online for six hours yesterday."

When working on the Internet, bring loads of self-discipline. Have a research plan. Naturally, it will require adjusting as you chase your data, but make sure that all of your efforts are leading you toward your goal. Take copious notes, and bookmark websites that look especially helpful. You *will* get there.

In this, and all your endeavors, I wish for you all the joy that life can give.

WHEN THE CUPBOARD IS BARE

While working at your job-hunt, you may find that it's taking longer than you ever imagined, and money is running low. If that's the case, consider signing up with one of the local temp services, and taking on some work. It may be a blow to your pride, but I can tell you from personal experience: you'd be surprised at what you can live with, and without, when times are desperate. And when times get even *more* desperate, you can be surprised again.

You might want to think again about craigslist, too. They have a section labeled "gigs," which are short, temporary jobs, often a godsend when money is tight. Maybe put up your own listing under "services," or in one of the "community" sections; take on some short-term work, do some consulting. Play your cards right, and you may end up with enough work that you won't need a traditional job.

SOURCES

Statistics about jobs

America's Dynamic Workforce 2006
2010 US Department of Labor

Sources of Hire 2008–2010
CareerXRoads

Weddle's—various reports
see www.weddles.com/

"The Career Networks," Forrester Research
www.forrester.com

"Stop Being Creative in Your Job Search," Net-Temps.com
www.net-temps.com/careerdev/career-tools/view-article.html?type=topics&id=3913
(also references statistics about television habits)

"New Unemployment and Productivity Numbers are Bad News for Job Seekers"
www.brookings.edu/opinions/2009/1106_unemployment_burtless.aspx

JObBait's Assessment of the Hidden Job Market
www.jobbait.com/a/hidden_job_market.htm

"5 to 1 Ratio Is a Mashup of Job Stats," Kathleen Bender.
San Francisco Chronicle, 7/15/10

"Job Seekers Facing Harsh New Reality," Alana Samuels.
San Francisco Chronicle, 9/14/10

Stats about jobs and job boards

Which Job Boards Have Good Hiring Success Rates?
http://www.veteranstoday.com/2005/07/18/which-job-boards-have-good-hiring-success-rates/

Pew Internet and American Life Project
www.pewinternet.org

"Best & Worst of Career Web Sites", Forrester Research
www.forrester.com

"Job Board Journalism: Selling Out the American Job Hunter," Nick Corcadilos.
www.asktheheadhunter.com/newsletter/OE20030617.htm

Effectiveness of various job-hunting methods

These are explored more fully in *What Color Is Your Parachute?* and *The Job Hunter's Survival Guide*, both by Richard Bolles, Ten Speed Press

Weddle's, various reports
www.weddles.com/

JObBait's assessment of Jobhunt Strategy Success Rates
www.jobbait.com/successrates.htm

"Job Search Methods and Results: Tracking the Unemployed."
Monthly Labor Review, 1992 (numerous subsequent studies on quoted data reveal no significant change)

Taylor Nelson Sofres Intersearch, reported by Andrea Coombes,
CBS Marketwatch 1/23/03

"US Job Recovery Pushes 30% Growth for Online Career Sites."
Nielson/Netratings 4/16/04

People

"The Strength of Weak Ties," Mark Granovetter.
The American Journal of Sociology, May 1973 http://smg.media.mit.edu/classes/library/granovetter.weak.ties/granovetter.html

Facebook/Social Networking

"The Many Facets of Facebook." *San Francisco Chronicle,* 1/1/11
www.sfgate.com/cgi-bin/article.cgi?f=/c/a/2011/01/01/BU601H20EI.DTL

Facebook Becomes Job Search Engine
http://recareered.blogspot.com/2010/06/facebook-becomes-job-search-engine.html

"The Facebook Fishbowl," Scott Harris.
Contra Costa Times, 6/7/10

Search Engines

"Ask.com Layoffs Spell Surrender," Brad Stone and Brett Pulley.
San Francisco Chronicle, 11/10/10

Texting

http://www.secretsofthejobhunt.com/profiles/blogs/texting-and-work-among-the

US Incarceration Rate

Wikipedia
http://en.wikipedia.org/wiki/United_States_incarceration_rate

Sidebar—Google Bombing

"'Miserable Failure' Links to Bush"
http://news.bbc.co.uk/2/hi/americas/3298443.stm

Wikipedia: Google Bomb
http://en.wikipedia.org/wiki/Google_bomb

Sidebar—A Bias Towards Language

Genome, Matt Ridley. Perennial (Harper-Collins) 2000, pp 94–5

Left gaze bias:
www.springerlink.com/content/b188227326337268/
www.smarterdating.org/face-reading-for-dogs/

Facial asymmetry abstract
http://dx.doi.org/10.1016/0028-3932(73)90049-3

Photos of facial asymmetry
http://www.upscale.utoronto.ca/PVB/Harrison/Parity/FaceStudy/FaceStudy.html

Sidebar—My Privacy Rant

Facebook's Zuckerberg Says the Age of Privacy Is Over
www.readwriteweb.com/archives/facebooks_zuckerberg_says_the_age_of_privacy_is_ov.php

Why Facebook Wants Your Email
www.technologyreview.com/web/26718/page1/

Facebook: All Your Stuff is Ours, Even if You Quit
http://mashable.com/2009/02/16/facebook-tos-privacy/

San Francisco Chronicle, 1/26/11: **Facebook's Ad Pitch Site to Convert 'Likes',
check-ins, other actions into revenue**
www.sfgate.com/cgi-bin/article.cgi?f=/c/a/2011/01/26/BU361HE35D.DTL

Contra Costa Times, 12/6/10: **Internet Needs a 'Do Not Track' Tool**
www.contracostatimes.com/ci_16761723?IADID

San Francisco Chronicle, 12/21/10: **Groups Hunt for Ways to Stop Tracking**
www.sfgate.com/cgi-bin/article.cgi?f=/c/a/2010/12/21/BUTT1GR464.DTL

Contra Costa Times, 1/17/11: **App Developers Can Get Address, Phone Number**
www.contracostatimes.com/business/ci_17120418

Sidebar—Our Resume Could Use Some Work:

Liars at the Ladders, Nick Corcadilos
www.asktheheadhunter.com/newsletter/OE20090120.htm

The Ladders Scam
www.jibberjobber.com/blog/2009/05/28/the-ladders-scam/

INDEX OF WEBSITES

INDEX

Government jobs, finding, 170
Granovetter, Mark, 90
Grants, finding, 171–173

Headhunters. *See* recruiters
Hidden job market and networking, 90
Holland Codes, 43–44, 45
Home business resources, 169–171
Hybrid resumes, 62

Indeed, 33–34
    Forums, 97
    networking and, 88
    Resume Tips, 73
Industry research, sites for, 130–131
Instruments, tests *vs.*, 43–46
Interviews, websites on, 167–168
Invisible Web, 123
Ireland, Susan, 63

Job boards, 8–9, 153–167
    effective use of, 161–162
    list of, 162–166
    networking and, 88–89
    problems with, 154–156
    recruiters on, 154
    resumes and, 12–13, 155–156, 162
    specialization in, 158–159
    websites for finding, 160–161
Job clubs, 115–116
Job-hunting methods and success rates, 12–19
Joyce, Susan, 16, 77

Keywords
    Resume Action Verbs and Keywords, 71
    in resumes, 66–68, 75–76
    Supersites using, 28
Knowdell, Dick, 46
Krueger, Brian, 21

Language, A Bias Toward, 89
LinkedIn, 93, 99, 101–102
    Answers, 104
    companies, researching, 137
    Company Profiles, 104
    Learning Center: Profiles, 111
    networking and, 89
    premium membership, 105
    Profile Extreme Makeover, 111
    salary data on, 147
    SimplyHired and, 33, 101–102
    toolbar, 104–105
    web persona for, 110–111
Linkup, 34–35, 88

Message boards. *See* Forums
Meyers–Briggs Type Indicators (MBTI), 40–41

Microsoft
    Office Web Apps, 74
    Word, resume writing with, 74
Minorities, researching jobs for, 145
Mobile technology, 9
Monster, 2–3, 28, 31
    job offers from, 14
    newspaper ads and, 36
    posting resumes on, 79
Mort, Mary-Ellen, 22, 26, 147
MySpace, 7, 93, 99, 107

Networking, 7–8, 16. *See also* Personal
        networking; Social networking
    approaches to, 88–89
    articles about, 91–93
    forums for, 94–98
    visibility, increasing, 111–112
    fatal flaw of sites, 91
    web persona and, 110–111
Newspaper want-ads, demise of, 36
Nonprofit Jobs, 143–144

Office Web Apps, 74
Older workers, researching jobs for, 145
Open Office, 75

Part-time jobs, researching, 144–145
PDF files for resumes, 76
People, 86–120. *See also* Networking
    companies, finding people in,
        141–143
    connecting with, 13
    core relationships, 90–91
    searching online for, 113–115
Personality testing, 40–43
Personal networking, 93
    information gathering with, 94
    websites for, 99–104
Personal web pages, 82–84
Portfolios, 81–82
Posting resumes, 78–80
Privacy issues, 109

The Quick Job-Hunting Map
    Prioritizing Grids in, 52
    skills assessment, 50

Recruiters, 15
    on job boards, 154
    resumes, sending, 84–85
    web persona and, 110
Research, 6, 121–152. *See also* Companies;
        Search engines
    databases, 125
    evaluating data from, 151–152